School's Out

WISDOM FOR NEW ADULTS ON INVESTING, LIFE, AND STANDING OUT IN A CROWD

C.J. MacDonald CFA

To Dylana, perfect every day, in every way. Without you, nothing is possible. With you, everything.

To my amazing children, Ryan, Lauren, Collin, Lucy and Kate. Although these lessons are meant for you, you have all already taught me more than you will ever know.

TABLE OF CONTENTS

PREFACE

Generation Z, those among us born after 1998, will soon outnumber the millennials, those people born between 1980 and 1997. Generation Z will comprise 32 percent of the global population of 7.7 billion in 2019, surpassing the millennials who will account for a 31.5 percent share. Generation Z will begin turning eighteen years old next year, meaning its members will begin to be voices on college campuses, in the workplace, and in the voting booth.

Generation Z does not watch traditional TV. If advertisers want to influence them, then they must reach into their phones. The people of Generation Z are the most digitally wired generation in history, and through their focus on YouTube, TikTok, Instagram, and Snapchat, they are wielding influence in global merchandising in ways unimagined only ten years ago. And contrary to what older generations fear about these young, uncommunicative phone zombies, they are in fact a very social, creative, and in-touch generation. Whether learning how to make crafts on YouTube, producing their own music videos on TikTok, learning how to influence consumers on Instagram, or following world events on Twitter, Gen Z is a very awake and informed generation that knows no boundaries between it and the outside world of entertainment, business and mentorship.

Generation Z has never known a non-digital world, and literally has instant access to all the world's news and information at their fingertips. However, even with so much available information, most do not know the important events that happened before their births. They do not know the basic financial terms and concepts they will need to understand in the real world. And they do not know why things are the way they are.

I have five members of Generation Z in my own at home; this book is full of the stuff I really think that they need to know as they venture out into the world.

CHAPTER 1

WHY TRYING AND FAILING IS SO IMPORTANT

A person would do nothing if he waited until he could do it so
well that no one would find fault with what he has done.

—Cardinal Newman

Eugène Boudin was a well-known art schoolteacher in Paris in the 1850s
and was a mentor to Claude Monet. On the first day of each school semester,
Boudin would divide his class into two groups for a one-month project. The
first group was told they would be judged on the *quantity* of paintings that
the group could produce in one month. The second group was told they
would be judged on the *quality* of one painting only.

At the end of the month, Boudin noticed consistently year after year that
the best paintings came from the group that focused only on the *quantity*
of work produced. Why? Because the quantity group, through voluminous
work, trial, and error, gained much more experience in the actual creation
of art. They were free to be creative, free to paint what they wanted to, and
free to gain experience from many attempts. They were unencumbered by
a goal of perfection. Basically, they tried and failed much more than the
other group.

The quality group, however, sat and pontificated about the perfect painting they wanted to create. They researched what the masters had painted

before them. They argued about what the painting should look like. They were stressed out about each brush stroke. Their goal was perfection, so they picked up their brushes to paint far less often. They did not gain the experience from trying and failing. That experience is what's needed to eventually create a great work of art.

An apprenticeship for a newcomer in any field can be a messy endeavor. Only by throwing a lot of paint at a lot of canvases, do we gain the experience needed to be able to create something truly great and unique later on.

Legend has it that Pablo Picasso was sketching in the park when a woman approached him.

"Oh, It's you! Picasso, the great artist! Oh, you must sketch my portrait! I insist," she said.

Picasso agreed to sketch her, and after studying her for a moment, he used a single pencil stroke to create her portrait. He handed the women his work of art.

"It's perfect!" she gushed. "You managed to capture my essence with one stroke, in one moment. Thank you! How much do I owe you?"

"Five thousand dollars," Picasso replied.

"What?" The woman moaned. "How could you want so much money for this picture? It only took you thirty seconds to draw it!"

Picasso responded simply, "Madame, that thirty seconds took me thirty years."

Masters in any field do not acquire their talents overnight. It is only through trial and error, continual learning, and failure that anyone gains the skill that is required to be a great master in a field. And inspiration is overrated. Professionals show up to learn and practice their craft every day. Amateurs in a field only show up when they are inspired.

A famous author was once asked about the role of inspiration in his writing labors. The author replied, "Yes, I do only write when I am inspired. But I happen to be inspired every day at 7 A.M."

Words of the Wise: There are no shortcuts. Only by continual practice in any field does someone become great. The people who show up day after day, attempting to do meaningful work, create enough mediocre work to get through to creating the good stuff. Show up. Do the work. Create. Learn. Fail. Then succeed.

CHAPTER 2

WRITE YOUR OWN STORY

Stephen Curry is an NBA superstar. He wears three NBA championship rings and owns two NBA MVP trophies. Curry is widely considered to be the best pure shooter in league history. Choosing Curry to start games at the best basketball colleges and as a number one pick in the NBA draft seems like an obvious choice now. But his road to superstardom did not begin under bright lights or with the cheering of adoring fans.

Curry was born in 1988, and is the son of a former NBA player, Dell Curry. Curry loved basketball from an early age and attended Charlotte Christian School in North Carolina. Curry excelled on the court in high school and was named to both the all-conference and all-state teams. He led his high school team to three conference titles and three state playoff appearances. But although he now stands six feet, three inches tall, Curry says he was always the littlest guy on his team growing up. He always felt like an underdog and constantly wanted to prove the naysayers wrong. As a high school freshman, he chose to not try out for the varsity team because he lacked the confidence to risk failure, and he regretted that choice by mid-season. He realized that he took the easy way out and vowed to never sell himself short again.

Because of his father's storied basketball career at Virginia Tech, Curry wanted to also play college basketball for the Hokies, but he was offered only a walk-on spot on the team. Smart basketball evaluators did not see hoops greatness coming from a short, wiry player with a skinny 160-pound frame, so he did not get much attention from the big college basketball programs. He ultimately chose to attend nearby Davidson College, which had aggressively recruited him beginning when he was in the tenth grade. Curry thought he deserved accolades and scholarship offers from the top basketball programs in the country, but those offers never came.

Curry confided to *MasterClass* in 2018,

> I didn't get recruited by any Division 1 schools and that was very frustrating. It was not a great feeling. I ended up at Davidson, which was a small school, and no one knew about them from a basketball standpoint. But I was able to create my own journey and write my own story there. I learned to appreciate the power and the beauty in that, and to embrace it. It taught me patience; it taught me to appreciate the opportunity I had, and that everything happens for a reason. And it taught me to fully embrace whatever your story is, and to make it yours.

Words of the Wise: For every superstar player that is recognized as brilliant at an early age, there are many more people that have had to work hard to overcome challenges and perceived shortcomings along the way. Every person is born unique, and everyone must appreciate the joy in writing their own story and walking the road of their own journey. Everyone's path to greatness is different. Make your story your own.

CHAPTER 3

WHAT IS INVESTING?

Saving money rather than spending it is surely the best way to grow wealth over time, whether you are a sixteen-year-old new-adult who has just secured a first job, or a sixty-year-old factory employee who has been working for forty years. You can only invest money and watch it grow in the future if you save some money in addition to spending it. If you have a dollar and have decided to save it instead of spending it, then good for you. But it is not a good idea to put that dollar in a drawer and leave it there for a long time. You need to actively invest it. But what is investing? What is the point of investing money, and what are the different ways to invest?

Investing is the act of using money to purchase an asset or to commit capital to a company, business venture, or real estate purchase. Investing is done with the expectation of generating an income or profit in the future. An investor anticipates that employing this capital now will allow the capital to grow as the business grows and generate profits as the value of the investment increases over time or as the investment makes interest payments. Purchasing an antique car that an investor expects to rise in value over time could be considered an investment. However, buying a new sports car is not considered an investment as its value is certain to decline over time if there are many similar models in the marketplace.

There are many ways to invest capital, but when making an investment an investor must strive to generate a return on that investment that clears two important hurdles. First, the rate of return on the investment must be higher than the inflation rate. Second, the rate of return must compensate the investor for the risk that he has assumed in making that investment.

An important concept to understand when evaluating an acceptable return on an investment is the rate of inflation. During most of the last two-hundred years in the American economy, price levels of goods and services have risen over time, which is called inflation. The rate of inflation today is low at about 2 percent a year, but even that moderate level of inflation will cause a dollar to be worth less over time than it is worth today. If a hamburger today costs $1 with a 2 percent inflation rate, then one year from today that same hamburger may cost $1.02. The dollar that you own can be used to buy a hamburger today, but a year from now it will not be enough as you will need $1.02 for that same purchase. In two years, that same hamburger may cost $1.04 and so on. If a bank pays a 2 percent interest rate on your deposit of that dollar, and the inflation rate is also 2 percent, then you are merely matching the inflation rate and are generating a real rate of return of 0 percent. The investor is not making any money but is not losing any money to the impact of inflation either.

Because of the negative effects of inflation, the minimum rate of return for the investment of a dollar is a rate that at least keeps pace with inflation. Inflation erodes purchasing power. If your ancestors put a dollar in a drawer in 1819 and you found that same dollar locked away in 2019, then it is still worth a dollar and you can spend it. That dollar may have purchased twenty hamburgers in 1819. In 2019 that dollar may only purchase one hamburger. That is how the effects of inflation diminish purchasing power over time. You must invest your dollars to generate a return that at least matches the rate of inflation to achieve an equal level of purchasing power over time.

The second investment return hurdle that must be met is that an investment must compensate the investor for the risk that the investor assumed by making that investment. Investment returns tend to be lower when the assumed risk is low and should be higher when an investment is risky. If an investor purchases a United States government bond, then payback of the principal of that bond is virtually guaranteed due to the good faith and credit of the United States government. However, due to the low level of risk, the interest rate that the investor will earn is low, around 2 percent in 2019. If an investment is made in an unproven oil drilling business venture, then the risk of loss is very high as it could be later discovered that there is no oil in that hole in the ground. Because of the higher level of risk, the potential return to the investor also needs to be high. As a basic rule, the higher the level of risk that an investor assumes, then the higher the return that an investor should demand and expect to receive. When investing money to generate a return on investment, there are no free lunches. If an investor desires a higher return on investment, then the investor must assume more risk.

As an investor, there are many ways for you to invest a dollar. You could save it and deposit it in a bank account where you would receive a small amount of interest for every day that the cash is at the bank. You could loan it out to someone else and receive interest on that loan until the principal is paid back to you. You could purchase a bond that's been issued either by a company or government entity, and you would receive interest on your investment until you sell the bond or it matures. All these investments of cash are loans. A bank account is the loan of your money to the bank for the time that your cash is at the bank. When buying a bond, you are loaning money to the issuer of the bond. Loans of this type typically carry a lower level of risk, so the return from lending your money to creditworthy entities is also low. While loaning money to others to earn a return on investment may be lower in risk, the return on investment that you will receive over time is capped as you will not receive more than the interest payments that were established at the time of the loan.

Or you could take that dollar and invest it in a business where you would become an equity owner of that business. You could open a lemonade stand where you would invest money to purchase the raw materials in order to sell your products. You would hopefully earn a return on your investment but only if your sales exceeded your costs. Or you could use your dollar to purchase a stake in another person's private company where you would assume part ownership of that company and receive your share of the profits of that business. Or you could use that dollar to buy shares of stock in a public company where its shares trade on a stock exchange.

Words of the Wise: While loaning money to others may offer a lower risk profile for the investor, the most powerful way to grow investment capital over time is to make investments in the ownership of a business. That is how the great fortunes of the world have been built and compounded in value over time. It's through the founding, growth, and profitable reinvestment of great businesses. Investing in the ownership of a business is certainly a riskier investment than loaning money to a bank or government, but the potential return to the investor is much higher. A new adult is blessed with a very long period in which to invest, and an investment in a business or the publicly traded stock of a business is the best way to generate and grow wealth over the long term.

CHAPTER 4

In the Mirror

"When you're twenty, you care what everyone thinks about you. When you're forty, you stop caring what everyone thinks about you. And when you're sixty, you realize that no one was ever thinking about you in the first place."

—Unknown

"You are dumb. Your hair looks crazy and you can't sing at all. You run slow. You're always late and your clothes fit you weird. Your hair doesn't fall right, and your nose is too big."

If an enemy spoke to you like this, then it would reconfirm why you two don't get along. If a friend spoke to you like this, then you probably would not continue to be friends with that person.

However, this is how we talk to ourselves every day in our own heads. The world can sometimes be a difficult and cruel place, but no one will ever talk to you as poorly as you talk to yourself. And no one will ever treat you as badly as you treat yourself. We tend to be harshly critical of our own perceived faults and imperfections while being forgiving or even totally unaware of the faults and tiny flaws of others. We judge ourselves far more harshly than the world around us judges us.

People also tend to overrate the qualities and talents that they do not have and largely underrate the great talents and attributes they do possess.

They do the same for what appears to be their natural-born talents, but came strictly from hard work.

I once watched a speaker address a large investment conference. He was passionate, engaging, and held the room in the palm of his hand for the whole hour. I thought to myself that this man must have been born a master of public speaking. He must have addressed his first-grade class with a thundering speech about juice boxes, cookies, and recess. And I thought there is no way that I could ever learn to speak that well.

The speech ended and I headed to a cocktail reception in the hotel bar. The speaker was also there, and I knew I just had to meet him, hear his story, and find out his secrets to life. I told him how much I enjoyed his speech and how in awe I was of his natural speaking ability. I said that I couldn't believe how he could just stand up in front of a thousand people and rattle off that interesting, passionate, and engaging lecture. The speaker listened to my comments and just laughed.

"That was the 327th time I have given that lecture" he said. "The first hundred times I was terrible. The next hundred were just okay. The next hundred were pretty good. But in these last twenty-seven tries, I have really hit my stride. You are seeing me at my peak. But thank you!"

The speaker was not a perfect public-speaking machine. He took one speech, practiced endlessly, tried, failed, stumbled, and repeatedly got back up to do it again. He learned which parts people liked and which parts made them yawn and check their phones. Now, all the audience sees is perfection. People only see him at his best. They missed the worst. But that worst does not matter now. Gaining worthwhile experience in any field takes a long time. And it takes a lot of patience, practice, failing, and character building.

You can only learn how to be a stand-up comedian by being on stage and failing many times until you know what makes people laugh. You can write jokes, practice in a mirror, and perform for your friends. You can test the jokes online. You can watch other comedians' videos and visualize yourself being on stage. But you will only become a successful stand-up comedian by taking the stage and doing your act. Again and again. Night after night. Boo after boo. Until you get it right. There is no other way.

Similarly, you cannot expect to be successful in any field without doing the hard work. Public speaking. Writing a book. Playing golf with a two handicap. Being a fashion designer. It all takes hard work, pain, and suffering to earn the skills and confidence that you will need to excel in a field.

Words of the Wise: These days with the all-consuming influence from social media, we continually compare our every day to others' highlight reels. We wake up in the morning and review new Instagram posts of friends or celebrities all dressed up, gorgeous, and living the life. Then we get out of bed and shuffle over to the bathroom mirror.

We say or think, "Yikes! I was very attractive last night, what happened to me?"

Do not compare another person's best to your everyday. Everyone struggles. Everyone has doubts. Everyone has insecurities that they battle. No one has all the answers. No one is perfect.

CHAPTER 5

STEP INTO THE SPOTLIGHT

Vivian Maier was an incredibly talented photographer. She stood nearly six-feet tall with short dark hair and had a penchant for hats and flowery dresses. She found joy in walking city streets snapping photos of everyday life. Critics raved about her artistic eye, technical skill, and the deep sense of human understanding that her work showcased. Her photographs have been seen and enjoyed in hundreds of galleries and exhibits around the world. The first show of her work at the Cultural Center of Chicago in 2010 attracted the largest crowds in the gallery's history. Vivian would have been rich and famous. But no one ever viewed or appreciated her art while she was alive. Not even Vivian.

Before her death, Vivian's prodigious work was unknown and unpublished, and most of her photographic negatives were never even developed or printed. Her talent and artistic savvy sat for decades in a Chicago storage unit, waiting for the world to discover what she had seen through her lens. What could have been a brilliant career was never to be. She died alone in 2009 at age 83, unknown, penniless and with no known heirs or assets.

Little is known about Vivian's life. She was born in New York City in 1926 to immigrant parents and as a child moved frequently between the United States and France with her mother. In 1956, at age thirty, she moved to Chicago and worked as a nanny for wealthy North Shore families for the next forty years. She was considered a loner, did not have any known family, children, or romantic life. She loved the children she cared for, however, and was later described by the children as a "real-life Mary Poppins." The children knew that Vivian had a sharp sense of wit, playfulness, and a quiet zest for living.

Vivian was a street photographer. Throughout her long life, she took hundreds of thousands of shots, most of them impromptu photos of people on the streets of Chicago and New York. She snapped haunting black and white photos of the homeless in doorways, construction men at work, children crying over spilled ice cream, couples kissing on a bus, dignified elderly ladies standing on a corner. Everyone was fair game for Vivian's lens, and her many works are as varied as they are extraordinary.

Most of her subjects had no idea that they were being photographed, nor were they aware that they were worthy of her attention. On a primitive Rolleiflex camera that she purchased in 1952, she took more than 150,000 photos over a period of forty years. She looked for subjects while wandering the city streets on her days off or while toting the children in her care. She walked for many decades. And looked. And snapped. Wandering with her ever-present camera hanging around her neck, Vivian felt most alive while taking photos of people and places in urban settings.

Unfortunately, her dazzling photos were undiscovered until 2007 when a young Chicago artist and collector, John Maloof, went looking for historical photos of Chicago's Portage Park neighborhood for a book he was writing. His search led him to the auction of an abandoned storage unit. The payments for the unit had lapsed, and it was for sale to the highest bidder. Maloof purchased a total of thirty-thousand of Maier's negatives for $380. He had no idea what he would discover in the faded and fragile cardboard containers.

When Maloof reviewed the large number of negatives and prints, he was shocked at the skill that he saw laid bare in the unknown photographs. Maloof eventually found the artist's name etched on one of the faded boxes. He searched the internet for Vivian Maier, but the search returned nothing. This singular artist was somehow unknown even to Google. Two years later Maloof found an obituary for Maier, who had died a few months before.

He sought out more Maier work, and purchased a large leather storage chest with hundreds of rolls of undeveloped film. Maloof eventually found additional old boxes of Maier's work, and he now owns 90 percent of Maier's total portfolio. His cache includes 150,000 negatives, more than 3,000 vintage prints, and hundreds of rolls of film, home movies, and audio tapes.

The reason that Maier's lifetime of work was never seen by anyone is unknown. She was described by people that knew her best as mysterious, eccentric, bold, paradoxical, and private. She must have realized that she was a skilled photographer, but for some reason did not need to see the results of her labors. Maybe she was so confident in her work that she did not need to see the end-product as validation. Maybe she loved the hobby of snapping photos but did not care for the business of art. Or maybe she was just too afraid of peer scrutiny to put herself in the public eye. We will never know the reasons that this artist did not recognize her own skill or aptitude, or why no one else was allowed to recognize it either.

Vivian Maier's tale of obscurity, despite being blessed with singular genius, is a sad one, but she is likely one of many. How many books over the centuries were left unwritten as the author could not summon the courage to tap the first typewriter key? How many inventions have been abandoned after the first few iterations failed to succeed? How many paintings were thrown in the trash, the artist deeming them unworthy of public viewing? How many great speeches went unspoken due to fears of standing before a crowd to allow one's voice to be heard?

Words of the Wise: What art are *you* capable of creating? What ideas are stored in your head that should be put on paper? What works of brilliance do you have inside you that could be appreciated by many? Will you keep your innate talents to yourself because you're afraid of a critic's glare, or will you offer them as gifts to humanity? At the end of your life, will a Google search of your name return nothing as Vivian's did? Will you sit quietly in the audience, or will you take life's stage and demand that the world pay attention to you?

You can be judged and perhaps criticized or you can be overlooked and ignored. The choice is yours.

CHAPTER 6

WHAT IS A STOCK?

The most basic concept in financial market investing is the ownership of a stake in a company. Buying a share of stock is also called owning an *equity* stake in a business, which is when a shareholder owns a part of that business. Private companies are all around you. A dry cleaner. A pizza shop. A chicken restaurant. These businesses are owned and run by one person or a small ownership group, and all business plans and financial information are private and can only be seen by the owners of the business. However, when a company wants to grow large and attract outside capital, it will register with the SEC and sell shares to the general public. Those shares trade on a physical or electronic stock exchange. After that registration and sales process, the company is now known as a publicly traded company. Why would a company want to be public rather than private? There are many reasons:

1) Capital: Selling shares in your business to the public helps to raise money that can be used to pay down the debts of the company and grow the business into new areas.

2) Shareholder base: Going public means that a much larger group of investors can have an ownership stake in your business. Other smart minds offering advice and caring about the growth and state of the business can aid the long-term health of the business.

3) Shares as currency: Publicly traded shares of your company can be used as payment for the purchase of other companies. Shares

of stock can also be used to compensate employees with a stake in the business.

4) Profile: Being a public company raises the profile of your company. The ups and downs of the shares are talked about by investors and by financial news and print outlets. Being a public company is usually thought of as more prestigious than being private.

Owning a share of stock in a public company gives the owner the right to a share of the profits of that company, which are usually received as regular dividend payments from that company. A shareholder also has the right to vote in corporate governance elections and the right to speak or ask questions of management at regular shareholder meetings.

If an investor wants to buy or sell shares of a stock, then he must open a brokerage account at a broker-dealer firm, such as TD Ameritrade, Vanguard, or Charles Schwab. A broker-dealer has technology links to all the major stock exchanges and will execute a trade in a public market on its client's behalf.

Shares of a publicly traded company are purchased and sold through a stock exchange and not through the company itself. While for centuries the New York Stock Exchange handled the majority of all trading of stock, in recent years the electronic exchanges have made great strides in capturing market share, and now trade a large amount of stock as well.

If an investor wants to purchase shares of stock in a company, then he must first learn the stock symbol of that company. Stock symbols are a short and easy way to differentiate one company from another. For example, Apple Corporation's stock symbol is AAPL. If an investor wishes to purchase shares of Apple Corp., then he will contact his broker or financial advisor either in person or access his online brokerage account, and enter a trade order that details the stock symbol, how many shares he wants to buy, and what is the desired purchase price. If the investor states that he wants his order to be a market order, then the trade will take place at the prevailing price in the market at that moment. If the investor places a limit order, then the investor states the highest price he will pay for that stock, and the trade will not necessarily take place immediately. The order will only be filled if he can buy the stock for his named price or at a lower price.

<u>Words of the Wise:</u> In the past, individual stocks were the primary equity investment vehicle utilized by average investors for investing in public companies. However, due to the invention and growth of newer products such as mutual funds, the index fund and the exchange traded fund (ETF), much of the investing done by clients both small and large is transacted through these cheap, simple, and convenient investment vehicles. Unless you have the time, knowledge, patience and risk tolerance to study, research, and trade shares of individual companies, most often the most prudent way to make periodic and consistent investments in specific market sectors or in the broad stock market is through mutual funds, index funds, and ETFs.

CHAPTER 7

THE WRONG SIDE OF THE TRACKS

You may not have noticed this odd fact before, but the dividing line in most cities between wealthy and poor neighborhoods is east and west. A large part of the population of the eastern areas of cities are less financially well-off and more disadvantaged than those in the western half.

The list of these cities is long, but includes East St. Louis, East Detroit, East Los Angeles., East Lansing, East Orange, and even East Palo Alto. This fact is similar in other countries as well as seen in East London, East Jerusalem, East Paris, and East Vancouver.

The global Industrial Revolution saw its origin around 1760 with the arrival of new technologies in key growth sectors such as textiles, iron, and steam. The consequences of that revolution were not realized until much later. The widespread use of coal as an energy source did not fully accelerate until the 1840s. There was a sharp increase in coal consumption between 1850 and 1910, and that is the period that saw the greatest growth in rural citizens relocating to cities. This period is when the east side/west wide residential sorting in major cities occurred.

Why did this sorting between the settling of the poorest citizens on the east side of towns and the richer folk on the west side of towns happen? It is because of the wind. The Earth rotates counterclockwise, so the wind in both hemispheres blows east. If you are setting up chairs around a campfire, then you should avoid placing your chair to the east of the fire if you don't like smoke in your face.

Heblich, Trew & Zylberberg released a fascinating study in 2016 titled *"East Side Story: Historical Pollution and Persistent Neighborhood Sorting."*

It was a geographical study of the location of 5,000 smokestacks in England in 1880. They concluded that because smoke blows to the east, the wealthier folks invariably settled on the west side of cities while the less powerful and more disadvantaged citizens were relegated to the east side. Many cities in America and around the world were settled in this manner as well.

The consumption of coal and its negative environmental effects were curtailed sharply after Britain's Clean Air Act was passed in 1956. The act introduced regulations that penalized the emissions of coal-produced pollutants. However, the settling and stratifications of city populations had already occurred and has been very difficult to reverse, even half a century later.

Words of the Wise: This is even where the term "from the wrong side of the tracks" came from. The wrong side of the tracks was usually the east side, which was where the smoke from the trains blew. Although pollution from trains, industrial plants and utility smokestacks have declined considerably since the 1800s, the demographic sorting effect in cities around the world is still visible.

CHAPTER 8

WHAT IS A 401(K)?

Before you land your first real job that offers a retirement plan, such as a 401(k), you need to learn about its features and start planning for your own future. A 401(k) is a retirement savings plan, sponsored by your employer. It lets workers save and invest a piece of their paychecks before taxes are taken out. The amount before those taxes are removes is called pretax earnings. You don't pay taxes on the money you contribute or the growth in that money until you take it out of your 401(k) account much later in life so that is a big benefit. You can elect to have a certain percentage of your paycheck deducted each pay period, and that money is contributed to your 401(k) account. Your account has your name on it, and you control it and how it is invested over time. Most plans offer many choices of mutual funds to invest in. Those are composed of stocks, bonds, and money market investments. How you invest the money in your account is up to you.

Learning how a 401(k) plan works is very important. That's because planning for your own retirement is your responsibility. In the past, workers could count on pension plans and social security payments to live a comfortable retirement. Not these days. It is now up to you, and no one can plan for your financial future except you.

A *company match* is also a very valuable feature to the growth of your assets. The company match is the amount that your company agrees to deposit into your account for your benefit. Many companies will match the money you contribute to your 401(k) account, and will do so up to a certain percentage of your income. The average match offered by companies as a benefit is 3 percent of your annual payroll earnings, but your company may offer a higher or lower percentage, so be sure to find out how much is offered. If you contribute 3 percent of a $50,000 salary into your 401(k), or $1,500, then your company will add another $1,500 into your account. You can add more than that $1,500 yourself, but the company won't match beyond that 3 percent. Always contribute enough to your account each year to at least receive the full company match. It is free money! And that company match will make a huge difference in the growth of your account balance over the many years before retirement.

There are contribution limits for 401(k) accounts, and for 2019, the maximum that you can add to your account in the calendar year is $19,000, not including your employer's match.

Why do we call it a 401(k)? In 1978, a chapter of the federal tax code (Chapter 401) was updated to include the creation, idea, and outline for these types of retirement accounts. The new 401(k) idea was an afterthought at the time, but soon grew quickly to be the main retirement planning vehicle for United States employees.

What if my company goes out of business? Not to worry as your 401(k) account and its investments are separated from your company's finances and debts, so even if your company hits hard times, your retirement savings are segregated and safe, and you can take your account to your next employer, untouched by your old employer.

How is a 401(k) different from a pension plan? Back in the old days, many companies used pension plans to attract employees and help them retire with a defined income until their death. With these so-called *defined benefit* plans, an employee's income after retirement was set in stone, and the employee knew what it would be and could depend on it for a secure retirement. A company would contribute an amount to the pension plan every year and would invest the funds to grow assets over time, and then pay out some of the funds every year to retired employees. In 1979, 32 percent of employees in the United States were part of a pension plan. However, today far fewer employees benefit from a pension plan, and are mostly government employees (police, teachers, firemen) and members of trade unions. Company usage of these pension plans have declined considerably over the years, and the responsibility for saving for retirement has been shifted to the employee through plans such as the 401(k).

A 401(k) plan is considered a *defined contribution* plan where only the amount of money added to a retirement account is known and with the ending account value dependent on the investments used, the amount added to the account over the years, and the amount of time the assets have a chance to grow. The amount contributed to the account is known, but the resulting financial benefits to the account owner is not defined as in a pension plan.

The days when pension plans secured a comfortable retirement for many employees are over, and these days it is an employee's responsibility to plan for his or her retirement, and to add and invest funds on his or her own. And beginning 401(k) contributions when you secure your first job can make a huge difference down the road.

For instance, let's say you earn $40,000 a year, contribute 10 percent to your 401(k) plan, receive a 3 percent match from your employer, and earn a 6 percent, average-annualized rate of return. If you begin making these contributions when you're twenty-two , then you would end up with over $1 million in your account by sixty-five. But if you had waited until age thirty to start saving, then you would end up with about $617,000 at sixty-five. Starting to save and invest at an early age is very important and could mean being able to retire earlier or live better in retirement with considerably more money.

Words of the Wise: Luckily, learning what you need to know to plan for a comfortable future is very simple, and you have all the tools and knowledge available to be successful. The most important principles for success are to start early, contribute consistently to the plan, and think long-term about your investment choices. If you do these three things, your chances of success greatly increase, and you will sleep well at night knowing your financial future is secure.

CHAPTER 9

DARE TO SUCK

"The brick walls are there for a reason. The brick walls are not there to keep us out. The brick walls are there to give us a chance to show how badly we want something. Because the brick walls are there to stop the people who don't want it badly enough. They're there to stop the other people. Not you."

—Randy Pausch, The Last Lecture.

Dan Brown is a talented and well-known author of thriller fiction books. He is the author of numerous number-one bestselling novels, including *The Da Vinci Code*, which has become one of the bestselling novels of all time. It's sold over eighty-million copies. Brown's novels are published in fifty-six languages around the world, with over 220 million copies in print. Brown has also been named one of the "100 Most Influential People in the World" by *TIME Magazine*.

Brown was kind enough to share his thoughts, experiences and guidance to teach a "Masterclass" on the art, science, and business of fiction writing. He fully described his writing process, how he approaches his craft each day, and the life lessons he has learned along the way. Brown specifically focuses in on the creative process, the constant grind of doing what he loves to do, and the trial and error that gets him to the ending of writing a bestselling novel. An interesting passage includes an interaction he had with a highly successful rock star:

Strangely, I learned a lot about creativity from someone who is very different than I am. A man named Steven Tyler, who happens to be the lead singer of Aerosmith. I had the experience of sitting next to him and talking about the creative process. And he told me that Aerosmith has this ritual of once a week having a band meeting called Dare to Suck. Dare to suck, I thought? What could this possibly be? And Tyler said, 'Each one of us brings an idea that we think is probably terrible, and that we are embarrassed that we even have the idea. But we present it. And nine times out of ten, the idea is actually terrible. But one time out of ten you get *Dude Looks Like a Lady* or *Love in an Elevator*.' And I thought to myself, 'That is an amazing way to approach the creative process. It is fearless.' So, when you are writing, or doing anything creative, dare to suck. Dare to be terrible first. Trust me, every single writer is bad sometimes. Those are all the parts of the book that they delete so that you don't have to read them. When you buy a book, you are not paying for the words on the page, you are paying for all the things that the author deleted that made the final copy great. You can always identify a serious writer by looking at the delete key on their keyboard. It is demolished. You can barely see the letters. It is just faded from hitting it so many times.

Creating anything of value in life takes struggle and perseverance and many bouts of trial and error. With all great works, we only see the final, perfect product. But there are always far more many versions that were thrown in the trash.

Words of the Wise: When you reach the point in any creative endeavor that you just want to stop and throw in the towel, you should consider that to be a truly exhilarating and transformative point. Because if you are at the point where you want to quit, it means that you are the point where everyone else that has gone before you also hit a wall and they chose to quit and turn back. This means that beyond this difficult obstacle there is very little competition;

the air is thin and the path has now cleared for you. Keep pushing. The top of the mountain lies just out of sight.

CHAPTER 10

THE ECONOMICS OF SUPERSTARS

Why do certain Hollywood actors, hip-hop artists, and professional athletes earn so much money? And why do the vast majority of other actors, music performers, and athletes struggle for recognition and earn so little?

Vilfredo Federico Pareto was born in Italy in 1848 and would go on to become an important educator and economist. Legend has it that he noticed that 20 percent of the pea plants in his garden generated 80 percent of the healthy pea pods. This observation caused him to think about uneven distribution of wealth and resources and his subsequent research indicated that 80 percent of the land in Italy was owned by just 20 percent of the population. He researched different industries and found that 80 percent of production typically came from just 20 percent of the companies. Pareto concluded that 80 percent of results usually come from just 20 percent of the action.

The *Pareto Principle* is also known as the *80/20 Rule*. It is the observation that most things in life are not distributed equally. For example, 80 percent of the world's wealth is owned by just 20 percent of the people. In business 80 percent of a company's total revenue typically comes from 20 percent of the customers. Also, 20 percent of workers generate 80 percent of the results. The 80/20 rule may seem like a random set of numbers, but examples can be found over and over in all fields and walks of life.

About 80 percent of Apple's profits come from 20 percent of its product line and 80 percent of Hollywood's total actor salaries are paid to 20 percent of its actors. That means 20 percent of the apps on your phone account for 80 percent of your usage. It means 20 percent of runway models earn 80 percent of industry earnings. How about the fact that 20 percent of fiction authors account for 80 percent of books sold? Or did you know that 80 percent of Kardashian wealth is owned by only 20 percent of all Kardashians? It's interesting that 80 percent of NFL player salaries are paid to only 20 percent of the players. Approximately 20 percent of Instagram accounts account for 80 percent of the total followers.

Just forty years ago, the global superstar economy was far more in its infancy than it is today. In *The Economics of Superstars*, Sherwin Rosen proposed that in 1981 there were two very important factors that needed to be present for the majority of wealth and benefits to flow to a small number of market participants. Rosen noted the phenomenon of superstars, wherein relatively small numbers of people earn enormous amounts of money and dominate the activities in which they engage. That phenomenon seemed to be increasing in the world even back then.

So, what does it take to become a superstar? For a few people to make a lot of money in a given field, it is necessary for the players to be differentiated and be subject to *imperfect substitution*. One pair of shoes at Target can be substituted for another, but LeBron James cannot be substituted with a rookie player. A Honda Accord can be substituted for a Toyota Camry, but Dwayne "The Rock" Johnson cannot be substituted with Harry Styles in a blockbuster movie. A McDonald's cheeseburger can be substituted for a Wendy's burger, but Taylor Swift cannot be replaced by the newest American Idol winner.

Joint consumption of a product is very important to those earning the most money in a field. Most of the spending in an activity flows to endeavors where there is a public consumption of the product and in which the artist or the goods producer puts forth the same effort no matter how many consumers enjoy the product. For example, a concert performer puts forth the same effort regardless of whether five people show up that night or five-thousand. An author writes the same book whether one hundred copies are sold or a million fly off the shelves. More simply, the costs of production do not rise in proportion to the size of a seller's market. This feature allows for scale in a market's sales as one record could sell ten copies or ten million.

It is also very important for the artist to be able to own the property rights to their product. A farmer can grow apples, but he does not own the rights to all apples of that type. If an artist creates a screenplay for a movie or writes a hit song, then the artist owns that product forever, or can sell the rights to a movie studio or music producer who may then pay a royalty to the artist.

Endeavors are especially lucrative where there is both imperfect substitution of products and joint consumption of a product. When these two attributes are combined, the possibility for talented persons to command both very large markets and very large incomes rises dramatically.

It is interesting that as Rosen proposed these ideas in 1981, he certainly had no idea of the scale or profitability that today's technology advances have made possible. In his summary, he wondered to his readers, "What changes in the future will be wrought by cable, video cassettes, and home computers?"

Rosen died in 2001 but surely would be amazed at the technological advances that have created the opportunity for massive earnings to a wide variety of product producers that now benefit from a staggering amount of scale. Products such as iTunes, Netflix, YouTube, Instagram, and Facebook all benefit from tremendous scale in all social strata in today's marketplace.

Words of the Wise: The advances of tomorrow are not known today, but the principles of scale and differentiation will continue to enrich a talented few producers that leverage these important market factors.

CHAPTER 11

PERFECTION IS THE ENEMY OF PROGRESS

I was not a great student in school. If I was very interested in a subject area, I did well. But if I was not interested in the subject, I did poorly. My short attention span for those subjects that I found boring did not make for a world-beating report card. But good grades aren't everything and a person can still do well in life without a stellar grade-point-average (GPA) in high school or college.

A study of seven-hundred millionaires showed that their average GPA was 2.9 and that valedictorians of high school classes go on to see much less success after graduation than those peers with more middling grades. This is because the skills that are rewarded in school, such as doing what you are told, are not valued as much in the job world and tend to hold workers and entrepreneurs back. Grades reward conformity and the willingness to work within a strictly designed system. Many brilliant students see their jobs as getting the best grades, but not in focusing on learning the material that is taught.

Karen Arnold, a professor at Boston College, performed a study in which she tracked the future success of a large group of high school valedictorians and salutatorians. From her study, she noted that while this group of high-GPA achievers did go on to do well in college and excelled at careers after college, there were very few risk-takers or world-changers in that group.

Arnold noted that in an individual field,

Even though most are strong operational achievers, the great majority of former high school valedictorians do not appear to be headed for the very top of adult achievement arenas. Valedictorians aren't likely to be the future's visionaries; they typically settle into the system instead of shaking it up. They're extremely well-rounded and successful, personally and professionally, but they have never been devoted to a single area in which they put all their passion. That is not usually a recipe for eminence.

After school ends, we all go on to work in fields that value true and specialized expertise. Learning to be a generalist in high school does not lead to the focused expertise that is later valued in most every field. If you are working as an accountant, then your boss does not care if you know history or science. Just balance his books.

Students who excel in traditional schoolwork do not necessarily love learning; they typically love excelling at getting good grades. The learning part of that is a byproduct. Arnold found that many kids who struggle in high school are interested and passionate about just one subject and want to spend a great amount of time on that subject to master it. This passion does not play well in the generalist grades department, so the stifling demands of traditional schooling can cause frustration in smart but focused students who just want to graduate and follow their passions.

School has clear rules to be able to succeed, but work life and pursuing a career after college does not. The real world is a much greyer environment where far different skills are rewarded. The ability to work with a team of peers. The comfort to take risks where the outcome is uncertain. The ability to speak in public and sell your ideas. The ability to envision the future of a market or sector. The ability to communicate clearly and be a leader. Sound judgement. These very valuable traits are not taught in school, but they can make the difference between big success and crushing failure later in life.

Eric Barker, an author who also writes the very popular *Barking Up the Wrong Tree* blog, says,

Following the rules doesn't create success; it just eliminates extremes – both good and bad. While this is usually good in that it eliminates downside risk, it also frequently eliminates earthshaking accomplishments. It's like putting a governor on your engine that restricts the car from going over 55 mph; you're far less likely to get into a lethal crash, but you won't be setting any land speed records either.

While dropping out of college to pursue a dream is not a recommended course of action, some of the most famous and wealthy businessman in the world have followed that path. The list is in fact long and distinguished: Bill Gates, Mark Zuckerberg, Thomas Edison, Richard Branson, Larry Ellison, Michael Dell, Steve Jobs, Henry Ford, Walt Disney and Andrew Carnegie. There is no such list that lays out the names of all the people who quit college and failed spectacularly. That list is surely long as well. Even so, the above list contains people who had a great business idea, knew they had to start the business now, and could not be constrained by the daily tasks of going to classes, scribbling notes and answering test questions.

Words of the Wise: If you struggle to meet expectations in school, then take comfort as you are in great company. School grades are not the only path to success in the world after school. Passion, interest, focus, entrepreneurship, a stomach for risk taking, confidence and perseverance are much more valued in the working world than simply being great at taking tests.

CHAPTER 12

WHAT IS THE S&P 500 INDEX?

The most commonly used and quoted measure that financial market professionals and investors use to follow the ups and downs of the United States stock market is the S&P 500 Index. The S&P 500 is made up of five-hundred large publicly traded companies that have stock listed on the New York Stock Exchange and other large United States stock exchanges. The S&P 500 Index is followed by investors as a gauge of the overall health and movement of the stock market in general. When an investor or commentator reports that "the market was up one percent today," they are usually referring to the day's gain in the S&P 500. The index recently traded at a level of 2,975 points. However, an investor does not need to understand how the index is calculated or even what 2,975 points means. The value for the average investor in following the index lies in tracking of the gains and losses for the broad stock market which the S&P 500 measures.

The S&P 500 is a *market capitalization weighted* index. A public company's "market cap" is simply the total current market value of that company. For example, Starbucks Corporation has 1.2 billion shares of stock outstanding. Each share recently traded at $96.25 per share. If we multiply the current value per share by the total number of shares outstanding, then we get a market cap of $115.5 billion. This means that if you wanted to purchase every share of Starbucks stock, it would cost you $115.5 billion.

There are 500 companies in the S&P 500 Index, but they are not all weighted equally in the index. Each company's weight in the index is determined by its market cap. For example, Microsoft Corp. has the largest market cap in the index in 2019 with a market cap of $1.06 trillion. Nordstrom

Inc. has the smallest market cap in the index at only $4.7 billion. Since the market cap of Microsoft is 225 times larger than the market cap of Nordstrom, Microsoft's resulting weight in the overall index is considerably larger. Microsoft is a much larger part of the United States economy than Nordstrom is, so its representation and weight in the index is much greater. Microsoft has a 4.3 percent weight in the S&P 500 while Nordstrom has only a 0.1 percent weight in the index. So, a 1 percent decline in the price of a Microsoft share moves the S&P 500 much more than a 1 percent decline in a share of Nordstrom. That makes sense as their sizes and weights in the index are so different from each other.

Words of the Wise: Many stock market investors who want to gain exposure to investing in large United States stocks (but do not have the time, expertise or ability to research and purchase individual stocks) can invest in the broad stock market conveniently and at a low cost by buying shares of an S&P 500 fund. With one small purchase of this type of index fund, the investor now has investments in all five-hundred members of the index. An index fund is a very quick, easy, and cost-efficient way to invest in the stock market. Making regular and periodic investments in an S&P 500 fund is a great way to invest in the United States economy and to grow wealth over a long period of time, and it is most often the best choice for a small investor.

CHAPTER 13

POCKET PASSERS AND SAVVY SCRAMBLERS

The investments you choose are far less important than your behavior while holding those investments.

A friend confided to me recently that while he has been adding money to his 401(k) account regularly and receiving his company's generous matching contribution, he has not looked at his account or reviewed his holdings in the last five years. He knows that he is invested in a variety of equity mutual funds, but he does not remember which ones. He sheepishly asked if he has made a mistake by not following the ups and downs of the market and his holdings regularly, and what he should do now to rectify his grave error of inattention.

I assured him that if he is making regular additions to his account, and new contributions were being invested in the equity funds automatically, then his lack of attention to the growth of his plan was actually a very positive thing. Inattention to a thoughtful wealth plan is a far better path to take than to be constantly reviewing, adjusting, and worrying about the account balance. A 401(k) is a long-term investment fund, and the investments do not require our constant attention like a child, a plant, or a pet does.

The secret to successful wealth building is simple. It's not what you specifically invest in that is important. It is how steadfast you are in staying on course with your plan over a long period of time. If your plan is to invest your 401(k) contributions in low-cost equity index fund, then that makes sense. Or you could choose to only buy stocks in the health care and consumer staples sectors as these sectors can ride out a recession better than broad-market exposure. That sounds fine too. You may decide to buy a mix of stock and bond mutual funds and reinvest all income. Good, go for it. Or you may hire an experienced financial advisor to create an asset allocation plan for you and then invest accordingly. That sounds smart as well.

But for the long-term success of any plan, the far more important factors than the details of the financial plan's investments are one's willingness and ability to stick with the plan through thick and thin. Through strong markets and corrections. And while enduring constant negative noise both from CNBC and your brother-in-law spouting end-of-the-world nonsense at Thanksgiving dinner.

In the NFL, many quarterbacks can drop back and complete a pass from a clean pocket. But great quarterbacks only get to prove their mettle when the pocket gets overrun with defenders and the passer must scramble and run for his life.

What type of investor will you be in the throes of a market correction when you feel like you are running for your financial life? Will you be like Jay Cutler, who frequently made terrible, game-changing decisions when flushed out of the pocket? Or will you be steady and thoughtful like Aaron Rodgers? Rodgers usually makes great decisions while under pressure and stress, with a confident, high-percentage pass, or by throwing the ball out of bounds to live another day, and make another play.

Like a clean pocket, it may be easy to navigate the equity market these days with confidence after enjoying a market rise of ten years in a row. However, the stock market will correct at some point, and investors will see paper losses in their accounts and feel the pain. Our economy will eventually slow and go through a recession. These slowdowns happen at least once a decade. Or there could be a political scandal that roils the markets, an armed conflict with another country, or a crippling trade war.

When these negative events will happen is not the question. *How* an investor behaves in these tough times is the factor that will make the difference between long-term investing success or failure.

<u>Words of the Wise:</u> All the smart portfolio and investing decisions that are made along the way can easily be undone if an investor lacks both patience and discipline while the markets are under temporary stress. What behavioral part will you play in your own investing success or failure?

CHAPTER 14

FROM THE PYRAMIDS
TO YOUR IPHONE

The ancient Egyptians never got to use iPhones, but they may have had a larger part in creating them than you would imagine.

King Tutankhamen, now known more often as King Tut, ruled Egypt as pharaoh for ten years until his untimely death at age nineteen. That was around 1324 B.C. King Tut was tall but frail and suffered the genetic ill-effects from severe inbreeding of the Egyptian royal family that was traditional and common over many generations. Recent examinations of his mummified body revealed that he had a clubbed foot and an infected broken leg at the time of his death. DNA from his mummy also revealed evidence of multiple malaria infections. A combination of these maladies may have contributed to his early death.

His reign was short and unremarkable, and his successors never acknowledged the reign of the boy king. King Tut was barely known to the modern world until 1922. That's when British archaeologist Howard Carter cut through an interior doorway and entered his tomb, which had remained sealed and undisturbed for more than 3,200 years. The tomb's vast hoard of 5,000 artifacts and treasures were packed from floor to ceiling. The possessions were intended to accompany the king into the afterlife. The tomb's treasures included furniture, chariots, clothes, jewels, weapons, and the king's royal walking stick. King Tut's solid gold coffin lay sealed and untouched.

When the tomb was opened in 1922, researchers found among the artifacts something peculiar and unexpected. There was a piece of cut glass, the centerpiece of a brooch that had been carved into the shape of a beetle. The piece of glass was later carbon-dated and was determined that it was created 26 million years ago, somewhere in the Libyan desert. Somehow the piece of glass, most likely created by a lightning strike into the desert sand, had made its way from the middle of an unending desert into the pharaoh's tomb. The brooch was the first known use of glass in ancient history.

While during most of human history, glass served only ornamental and decorative purposes, its use in recent centuries has revolutionized technology, medicine, astronomy, and education. Glass was a key factor in the rapid increase in the upward trajectory of human knowledge over that time.

Glassmakers during the Roman Empire learned how to make glass that was both clearer and more durable than earlier, less useful versions. Glass windows were created and used during this time because the knowledge and process of melting silica into glass became more refined. Glass was also commonly used during this time in drinking vessels, wine bottles, glasses, ornamental jewelry, and decorative vases. But the world had to wait until the next millennia for glass to evolve into what it is today: one of the most versatile and transformative materials in human history.

Monks in the twelfth and thirteenth centuries used curved chunks of glass to read religious texts in candlelit rooms. Somewhere around this time in northern Italy, glassmakers first created small glass disks that were thicker in the center than at the edge. They then attached wire to the two disks to create a frame, and the first eyeglasses were born. For many years after, only monastic scholars used the new eyeglasses. That's because they were the only members of society who were literate. Many other citizens were farsighted, but were unaware of their poor vision as they had no occasion to read anything, and their farsighted condition did not affect their normal everyday routine. People who could not read had no cause to squint at tiny letters on a page.

What marked a major turning point in the history of glass, science, technology, and the education of average citizens was Gutenberg's invention of the printing press in the 1440s. The printing press, and the much wider availability of the written word, caused literacy rates to rise dramatically. Suddenly, religious texts, novels, schoolbooks, and biographies were now in the hands of the common citizen. New theories of existence and science flourished and were published in books. Children could now read history in schools. Libraries could now offer wide access to books, texts, and other reading materials never seen before by the average person. Prior to the invention of the printing press, written materials were exclusively used by the church. Common folks were unable to communicate any new ideas of science, political, or religious beliefs that went against church teachings. The printing press democratized human thought in ways never seen in human history.

There was another important discovery that Gutenberg's invention set in motion that was much less appreciated at the time but was as important as the printing press. Now that the mass of society realized that they had poor vision and required eyeglasses, the popularity of eyeglasses focused many inventive and creative scientists on working with glass to improve its quality and chemistry. Within a hundred years of the invention of the printing press, thousands of eyeglass makers around Europe were running thriving and profitable businesses, and eyeglasses became the first piece of wearable technology that the average person would commonly use.

But the innovation would not stop there. The invention of eyeglasses not only focused great scientific minds on just improving eyeglasses, it focused great thinkers on all the other possible uses for glass. In 1590 Dutch eyeglass makers experimented with lining up two lenses on top of one another to magnify the effect on a tiny spot. The microscope was born, Within a few decades, scientists were publishing textbooks with hand drawings of what they had seen under their microscopes. Scientists for the first time had a clear vision of a single living cell, the building block of life. The study of microbiology was born.

The telescope was invented shortly after the microscope, and Galileo soon got word of this amazing invention and modified his model to increase the vision of his telescope to ten times normal vision. Within just two years of the telescope's invention, Galileo used his telescope to view the moons circling Jupiter. It was 1610. His vision certainly upended the common notion that all the planets revolved around the earth and revolutionized the interest in and study of astronomy.

Over the next few centuries, the development of the many uses of glass increased exponentially. Photography, the television, carbon fiber airplanes, fiberglass circuit boards, and iPhones are all clever and highly manufactured uses of simple glass. Today the backbone of the global internet is built on a worldwide array of fiber-optic cables, each made up of thin strands of glass stretched across oceans and around the world.

Words of the Wise: The next time you take a selfie, look in the mirror, or watch a YouTube video, remember that these products have their origins in the sands of the Sahara Desert millions of years ago, and the use of glass evolved over four millennia from the diligence and creativity of the human mind.

CHAPTER 15

WHAT IS A BOND?

A bond is a contract between a borrower and a lender. A bond represents a loan made by an investor to a borrower. Bonds are used by companies, municipalities, states, and sovereign governments to finance projects and operations. The contract states how much money is being lent, for how long, and how much interest the borrower must pay the lender over the loan period. A bond can also be referred to as a fixed-income security. That's because the amount of interest that a bond owner receives over time is fixed and cannot be changed.

Let's say that you think that Apple is a great company and feel comfortable lending the company your money for its use as it sees fit. You do some research and discover that Apple will sell new ten-year bonds in a bond issuance tomorrow. Apple will sell these bonds with a coupon yield of 5 percent. Great, you say, and you then purchase $100 in ten-year Apple bonds. At the end of each year for the next ten years, you can expect to receive interest payments of $5 (a 5 percent yield). And at the end of the ten-year life of the bond, Apple will pay back your original principal of $100. It's simple. If you held the bond for the entire ten years and you never tried to sell the bond in the meantime, then you would not know or care if the bond's price in the market had gone up or down.

However, if after two years you had decided to sell the Apple bond, then you would discover that the price of the underlying bond may have changed since you purchased it for $100. Let's say that in those two years since your purchase that interest rates had risen, and new ten-year Apple bonds were being sold with a 6 percent coupon rate.

"Wow," you think. "Why would anyone want to buy my bond paying a 5 percent rate of interest when new similar bonds are paying a 6 percent rate of interest?"

The short answer is that they would not. Unless you sold the bond for a cheaper price that made up for the difference between your bond with a 5 percent yield and new bonds yielding 6 percent. In order to make your bond equal to a higher yielding bond, and therefore be an equally attractive purchase as the new bond, the price you sell it for needs to be lower than your original purchase price.

Your bond yields 5 percent (you receive $5 a year in interest, dividend by your purchase price of $100, equals 5 percent). When you look up the current price of your bond, you find that the price has declined to $83. This is the price that makes the yield on your bond equal to the yield on the newer bonds. To determine this take the $5 a year that you will receive in interest, divided by $83, which equals a 6 percent yield. Your bond will only sell in the market if it is priced at $83 or lower as this is the price at which investors would see no difference between your 5 percent bond and a newer 6 percent bond.

While the sources of performance return from stocks come from corporate earnings growth, dividend payments, and multiple expansion, the long-term return on bonds is much easier to predict. When you purchase a bond, how can you estimate the yearly return that you will receive from that bond if a bond's price constantly moves in the marketplace? Studies of the last hundred years have shown that 91 percent of a bond's total return over time is directly related to the stated yield that you receive on the day you purchase the bond.

If you buy a bond and rates in the market rise, then you would have a paper loss on the now lower price of your bond. But that loss would be offset. That's because you would be able to take your interest payments from the bond and invest them at the new higher rates in the market. Alternatively, if rates fall in the market after you purchase your bond, your higher-yielding bond would become more valuable, but this gain would be offset as you invest the interest payments from your bond at the now lower market rates. Therefore, capital gains and losses barely register as a source of positive or negative performance over the long term in bond investing. Today, the yield on an Apple company bond is 4.2 percent, so that may be a very accurate prediction of an Apple bond investor's total return over time if the bond was purchased today.

Words of the Wise: Bonds are purchased by investors for the primary purpose of receiving the income that the bond generates from interest payments. Bonds are usually considered to be a less risky investment than stocks as their prices are less subject to the daily price swings that affect stocks. Bonds trade more with the overall level of interest rates than with the volatile swings of the fortunes of the underlying company. Bonds represent a debt of the underlying company as opposed to an ownership stake in the company that a stock investment represents. Bonds have ratings, indicating the quality of the underlying issuing entity and the riskiness of the entity paying back the principal at maturity. These ratings range from AAA, the highest quality bonds, to C, the lowest quality bonds.

CHAPTER 16

Don't Ask for Help. Ask for Advice.

Consider these two situations. You are at a party and a man walks up to you and introduces himself. After a few pleasantries, he inquires, "I am looking for a job. Can you help me find one?" You meet another man later that night who asks, "I am looking for a job. Do you have any advice for me?"

Which person would you most feel like helping? The first man wants to put a difficult task on your to-do list. It's a task in which you can either succeed or fail. And it's an added chore that does nothing for you, your happiness, or your life. However, the second man appears to have assessed you as someone who could help him with good advice, which strokes your ego. He also has asked for a favor that you can grant immediately by giving him your opinion with no future obligations. And he has given you a chance to impress him with who you know and what you know.

People love to give advice, but far fewer desire to be inserted into your life to help you. Asking for help makes it appear that you want to take something from the asked. Asking for advice, on the other hand, offers the opportunity for the person who has been asked to give something valuable to the person asking. That is a rather large distinction. People feel good when they give gifts to one another. But people feel bad when they feel that something is taken from them, such as time, productivity, or future focus on their own busy lives.

Asking for help also implies that only the person asked can be of service to the asker. But asking for advice may cause the advisor to open his mental contact list to consider who in his vast network of contacts could help this person.

A conversation may unfold like this.

"I am looking for a job. Do you have any advice for me?"

"Well, what kind of job are you looking for?"

"I studied film in college, and I really want to work on a movie set".

"Interesting. I own a plumbing supplies company. But my best friend from high school is a movie producer. Here is his contact information. You should call him".

It is always surprising the number of people that the average person knows and can direct you to if you just ask them in the correct way. The advisor helped the job seeker with contact info, so he feels good and has no further obligation. The job seeker now has a valuable new contact to ask for further advice. It's a definite win-win outcome.

Words of the Wise: Although Mom may have told you to never talk to strangers, you are older now. You need to start talking to strangers. Each person you see has a vast knowledge of subjects that you do not and a long list of contacts that you lack. Talk to strangers. Lots of them. In line at Starbucks. While sitting on a plane. While in line at the post office. You will be shocked at what people know and who they know. And these days, sizing someone up by what they look like or what they are wearing is not helpful. In the old days the man in the suit and tie was connected and powerful and the guy in the flannel shirt was not. These days, technology billionaires wear hoodies and jeans. You never know who you could be about to talk to. Conversations with strangers are never a waste of time and could be very valuable to your future and personal network.

CHAPTER 17

RISE AND FALL OF A
RETAIL LEGEND

In 1980, Nobel-prize-winning economist Milton Friedman visited *The Phil Donahue Show,* a television talk show, for a wide-ranging discussion of economics, free-market theory and the current state of the economy. During his highly decorated professional life, Friedman was an unabashed champion for the benefits of free-market capitalism and *the invisible hand,* the unintended social benefits of an individual's self-interested actions. While Friedman was at times seen as a fan of big business, he frequently denied that accusation, stating instead that he was not a proponent of large companies, but he was only a supporter of the power of the free enterprise system in general. He also firmly stated that he was a champion not of economic fairness but in economic freedom for all people.

The large players in the retail store industry were of course very different in that era almost forty years ago, and Friedman and Donahue engaged in a discussion regarding large department store chains and the acquisitive nature of large American businesses. They also discussed powerful and growing companies and the potentially harmful effects of monopolies on the free enterprise system. Sears was an American business stalwart as it was the largest retailing chain in the nation and had been for forty years.

"So, you are saying Sears can buy Kmart if they wanted to?" Donahue challenged.

"Of course, they can," Friedman replied, "but if Kmart keeps growing like it has been, Kmart may end up buying Sears!".

Seen through the lens of almost forty years of business evolution, the debate involving these two store chains seems quite quaint and humorous now. The business marketplace has always been characterized by continuous dynamic change and certainly has been since this debate. Walmart was not even part of that discussion. Neither was Costco. Neither was Target. Walmart's place in consumers' lives grew strongly after tapping into consumer preference and needs and the firm grew to overtake Sears as the largest retailer in the world in 1989. Costco pioneered the membership-club store model in 1983 and is now the world's second largest chain of retail stores. The first Target store opened in 1962, grew its store base strongly in the 1980s and 90s, and is now the third largest retail chain in the nation. Amazon, today's internet retail giant, was not even a glint in corporate America's eye in 1979. It opened its website in 1995.

In free-market capitalism, the quick and the smart usually beat the slow, complacent, and unimaginative. There is no greater example of this principle than Sears, which declared bankruptcy in September 2018. It is in the slow process of winding down its operations.

Sears, Roebuck and Company was founded in 1893 as a mail-order catalog for Midwest consumers who lived far from stores. Sears opened its first retail stores in 1925 and grew its store base quickly through the 1970s. A staple in our country's retail consciousness for decades, Americans shopped at Sears for Toughskins jeans, Kenmore appliances, and Craftsman hardware tools. Customers waited at their mailboxes for the annual Sears Christmas catalog and got their autos repaired at a Sears Auto Center. Sears was the largest retailer in the United States until 1989. That's when the rise of specialty stores, the convenience of online shopping, and a loss of corporate focus while diversifying into unrelated businesses such as finance, all combined to lead to Sears' slow downfall into oblivion.

Sears was forced into the bankruptcy liquidation process in 2018 as there seemed to be no hope of reviving the store chain in a vastly different consumer world than it grew up in. But the constant change in the retail landscape marches on. Many of the owners of malls where Sears have stores could not have been happier. Mall owners with trendy retailers, popular restaurants and new entertainment venues continue to evolve and prosper, even in a time when many store chains have closed their doors. Many of these landlords welcomed Sears' departure. The stores' exits allowed them to take over these big-box spaces and lease them to a more profitable tenant. In malls where leases were signed decades ago, Sears' rents were as low as $4 a square foot. New tenants in the same space could bring as much as six times that amount.

Although the failure of a large company like Sears may cause creditors to lose money, force unemployment on their workers for a short time, and cause the physical assets to lie dormant for a time, a corporate bankruptcy is simply the pruning of the free-market tree. Creditors will write-off the losses and re-focus attention on their more profitable loans. Employees will find new jobs with new companies or in new industries. And storefronts, manufacturing plants, equipment, and brands will be purchased by more profitable companies and revamped for new purposes. This creative destruction is at the heart of a dynamic free market system. Since the founding of our country, it always has been and always will be.

Over time many folks have worried that large companies may wield too much economic leverage in the market and have too much power over consumers and Congressman. However, being a large company does not save a business from bankruptcy as was shown in the cases of Sears, Chrysler, General Motors, and Penn Central Railroad. It may seem as if large businesses enjoy positions of great power, but a business cannot get a dollar from a consumer unless he hands it over willingly. All these businesses discovered that. The bigger they are, the harder they fall. Friedman did not fear corporate monopolies. He said instead, "The best anti-monopoly legislation you could have is completely free trade." He was convinced by history that the market could take care of itself. The businesses that served consumers best would rise, and those that did not would falter.

Chrysler Corp. filed for bankruptcy in 2009 during the depths of the global financial crisis of 2008-09, but it also had a near-death experience in the late 1970s. Chrysler was only saved from bankruptcy at that time by a government bailout package that was passed by Congress in 1979 to keep Chrysler in business. The debate over the wisdom of that government intervention was raging when Friedman was a guest on that *Donahue* show.

Donahue challenged Friedman on why it was not a good idea for the government to step in to save Chrysler:

Friedman noted, "The government should not help to save Chrysler, of course not. This is a private enterprise system. It's often described as a profit system but that's a misleading label. It's a *profit and loss* system. And the loss part is even more important than the profit because it's what gets rid of badly managed, poorly operated companies. Chrysler ought to be allowed to go broke."

Chrysler was able to avoid bankruptcy in 1979, but it would not in 2009. The government did not step in to throw it a lifeline the second time, and the company went through bankruptcy, reorganized, discontinued some brands and products, and re-emerged as a stronger company. But that was only because consumers still wanted to buy Chrysler autos.

Sears is dead and gone due to the rapid and savage changes in the retail sector that it did not or could not keep up with. Sears did not lose its edge overnight. There was not one moment that it missed or one decision that sunk the once proud company. It took decades for the slow drip of time, inaction, and missed opportunities to doom the company to the ashbin of avoidable business failures.

Words of the Wise: Who knows. In forty years from today, we may look back and lament the slow slide of Walmart, Target, or Costco, who were bested by a new company founded this morning that no one currently knows about but will continue corporate America's never-ending march of change.

CHAPTER 18

GO BIG OR GO HOME

In the last fifteen years, there has been a revolution in the NBA where on-the-court players attempt their shots. The Golden State Warriors are the subject of a lot of headlines these days for its remarkable shooting efficiency and its focus on the three-point shot, but the evolution of NBA scoring is seen widely in all NBA teams' stats. In the 2018-19 season, the average NBA team is attempting an astounding thirty-two three-point shots per game. That's compared to only fifteen three-point shot attempts per game in the 2003-04 season.

The Houston Rockets relies heavily on the efficiency of the three-point shot. In the 2018-19 season, its players attempted three-point shots at an incredible rate of forty-five per game while making 36 percent of these shots. In the 2008-09 season, only one NBA team scored an average of ten or more three-pointers per game. This season, two-thirds of teams are converting three-point shots into points ten or more times per game. Just ten years ago only seven of thirty NBA teams attempted more than twenty three-point shots per game. Now all the teams are attempting at least twenty, and the NBA average is more than thirty three-point attempts per game. Shooting three-point shots at a 40 percent success rate gives a team a higher average point score per possession, and that slight advantage is large when spread over one hundred possessions per game.

Scoring analysis shows that the most inefficient shot a player can attempt is in the area between sixteen feet from the basket and the three-point line. It is for this reason that in today's game you will frequently see a player with a wide-open, seventeen-foot shot pass the ball out to a player beyond the three-point line to attempt a shot. Although the team is choosing to take a much lower percentage shot, the attempt is more efficient at scoring points over an entire game. This season only 8 percent of superstar shooter Steph Curry's shots come from this inefficient area. That's down from 30 percent a decade ago. Teams now routinely only shoot from eight feet or closer to the basket, or from beyond the three-point line. NBA teams have decided that "go big or go home" is the only way to play the game.

While the concept of "go big or go home" may be a new paradigm for the NBA, for stock market investors this all-or-nothing nature of equity returns has been around as long as the stock exchange itself. While most investors do not realize it, the stock market over the past hundred years has generated returns in this same "go big or go home" manner. While the S&P 500 shows average annualized returns of more than 9 percent a year over this period, the actual results are very much "go big or go home." Like the eighteen-foot NBA shot, a calendar year return in the range of 0-10 percent is very rare as a yearly return in this range has only occurred in 15 percent of all market years. Much more likely is the "go big" range of market gains (more than 10 percent in a year) as we see these large returns in 60 percent of all market years. More common than 9 percent gain years are years in which stock market performance is below 0 percent; these are seen in 25 percent of all years.

In some years, stocks rise far more than anyone expected, and sometimes stocks fall much more than expected. In 2009, during a crippling recession and at a time when sentiment about the future of the United States economy and the stock market was at its most negative, stocks rose 26.4 percent. In 2018, in an economy with strong corporate earnings growth, low unemployment, high consumer confidence, and low inflation, stocks declined. They were down 5 percent. Nobody is an expert at predicting the direction of the stock market in the short term, so you should not try, or even listen to, seemingly smart folks who claim they have more vision about the future than a Magic 8 Ball.

While it would be far more pleasant to simply chug along every year enjoying stock market returns of 9 percent, the market has a mind of its own. The stock market went big in 2013, gaining 32.4 percent, but went home in 2015, rising only 1.4 percent. The market went big in 2017, rising 21.8 percent, but went home in 2018, losing 5 percent. It may be frustrating that all these years are considered normal equity market performance, but that is the cold reality of stock market investing, and is what makes it so confounding, interesting and rewarding for patient, long-term investors.

Words of the Wise: To enjoy the years when the stock market goes big and delivers strong returns, an investor must stay strong and persevere through the years in which the market performs poorly as it did in 2018.

CHAPTER 19

THE LESSONS OF THE VANDERBILTS

"I AM NOT DYING!" came the thunderous retort from the Commodore in the upstairs bedroom. "The doctor says I will be well in a few days! And even if I *was* dying, I should have vigor enough to knock this abuse down your lying throats and give the undertaker a job!"

On May 10, 1876, fans, well-wishers, and reporters had gathered outside the stately Fifth Avenue mansion of the richest man in the world, Cornelius Vanderbilt. He was 82. Word had spread that the health of the old man, long ago nicknamed "the Commodore," was failing, and the end of his glorious life was near. Like vultures waiting to prey on the carrion, his large family, including his ten children, had gathered downstairs to await the death of their perennially cranky father. Each of them had inquired about the state of the will that day, hoping to get advanced word of who he would favor with his riches. His close family had long suffered the slings, arrows, insults, and caustic comments of the Commodore. They were waiting for their monetary rewards. Vanderbilt was one of the richest men in the country. He had an estimated fortune of $100 million, which would be worth more than $3 billion today. However, the Commodore had no interest in dying that day and even less interest in leaving large sums of money to his unproductive and ungrateful children.

Vanderbilt was a self-made multimillionaire and built his fortune while dominating both the ferry shipping and railroad industries in the 1800s. With little interest in school as a boy, he labored with his father who operated a cargo ferryboat between Staten Island, New York, and Manhattan. After working as a steamship captain, Vanderbilt went into business for himself in the late 1820s. Through cutthroat business machinations and brute force, he eventually became one of the country's largest steamship operators. In the 1860s, he shifted his focus to the railroad industry. That's where he built another large empire and helped make railroad transportation more efficient and widespread. Over the years, Vanderbilt gained a well-earned reputation for being fiercely competitive, ruthless, and someone you did not want to cross paths with. He once wrote a letter to a team of business partners who he felt had wronged him, saying only "Gentlemen: You have undertaken to cheat me. I won't sue you, for the law is too slow. I'll ruin you."

Looking back, the story of the vast Vanderbilt fortune is a cautionary tale for all wealthy people, their heirs, and their estate planners. Vanderbilt did pass away the next year and his large estate was distributed to his unworthy (in his eyes) children. The children did prove their unworthiness at growing their vast inheritance into the future and ensuring the financial security of Vanderbilt generations to come. After Vanderbilt's death, his heirs attempted to solidify their place in noble society by spending vast sums of money on parties, yachts, country homes, and mansions. The ten Vanderbilt mansions that were built after his death lined Fifth Avenue in New York City. Each one was more ornate than the next and did not serve future generations of family members. The first mansion was completed in 1883, and the last one was torn down by 1947. The Commodore's vast fortune was squandered within thirty years of his death. By 1907 no member of the Vanderbilt family was among the richest in the United States. Within forty-eight years of the Commodore's death, one of his descendants died penniless. When 120 of Vanderbilt's descendants gathered at Vanderbilt University in 1973 for a family reunion, not one of them was even a millionaire. The old saying is "shirtsleeves to shirtsleeves in three generations," and that was certainly the case with the Vanderbilt family.

Although the rapid decline in the Vanderbilt fortune is a well-known cautionary tale, if we look below the surface of the story, then there are far greater lessons to be learned other than "Don't leave your money to your idiot kids." Children do not grow up in a vacuum and only learn the lessons that their parents teach them. They only mirror the example that their parents set while in their sights. While it may be easy to lambast the Commodore's children for squandering his fortune, they only knew what he had taught them. And he made many mistakes along the way that led to the ruin of his fortune and legacy.

First, Vanderbilt was a profane and surly man, husband, and father. He was highly competitive and insecure, and no one, not even his own children, measured up to his lofty expectations. He constantly berated his two only sons, Cornelius and William, with insults of both their intelligence and worth. "Blatherskate! Sucker! Stupid blockhead! Chucklehead! Beetlehead!" were the common admonishments of his namesakes. Constantly tearing down the self-worth of those who will inherit your fortune is not a great way to ensure the success of your future generations and your estate plan.

Second, his children never learned anything about business or how to handle money. He never taught them. His sons were a constant disappointment in his eyes, and he had even less use for his eight daughters. One by one, his daughters married and took their husband's names. To the Commodore, they were "not real Vanderbilts any longer." If a wealthy person does not pass on any wisdom that he has learned to succeeding generations, then it is no wonder that they do not possess this knowledge later when it is most critical and needed. His children were born with the Commodore's genes but did not naturally possess his wisdom. He failed to purposely pass this wisdom on, and his hard-won fortune could not survive this negligence after his death.

Third, the example that the Commodore set during his later years set the stage for the outlandish spending that would occur after his passing. The Commodore rose from the depths of the gutter, becoming one of the wealthiest men in the world, and he ached to climb up into high society to prove how far he had come in life and to stick it in the face of New York's higher class. He threw lavish parties fit only for the newly rich Gilded Age in which he lived. He built huge country and ocean-side homes and threw money around as if there was no tomorrow. Vanderbilt had no interest in anything but making money and showing the world that he had arrived. His children surely watched, learned, and waited for their turns at the checkbook.

Lastly, while Vanderbilt did bequeath his vast fortune to his heirs, he did not make his wishes known as to what he wanted them to do with their new wealth. The best estate plan in the world, prepared by the most careful and expert lawyers and financial planners, cannot survive the death if a family patriarch or matriarch are silent on what they desire their financial legacy to be. What charities they want to continue to support, what causes matter to them, what traditions they wish for the family to continue, what their hopes and dreams are for the family after they have passed. Heirs do not know this information just by being born with the same last name as the wealth-gatherer. This post-death planning must be as detailed and well thought out as the actual estate planning if the family's hard-fought legacy is to last more than one generation.

Words of the Wise: There is much more involved in successful estate planning than deciding where the money goes. While the Vanderbilt story is a sad one, it can teach the parents, children, and estate planners of today some very valuable lessons.

CHAPTER 20

Out of the Darkness

Melkemu was a 14-year-old boy from Arba Minch, Ethiopia on the day he walked out of the darkness. Melkemu was tall, lean, and scared as he entered the eye surgery center that morning in November 2017. Melkemu had been blind for seven years with a form of pediatric cataracts that can be caused by malnutrition or heredity. Melkemu dropped out of school as a small child when he could not see well enough to do his schoolwork, and the other children made fun of him. Without anyone to care for him during the day, he followed his father to the fields where he worked. Melkemu sat there by himself in the field all day, waiting for his father to finish his toils.

This day, however, was to be a much brighter day in many ways for Melkemu. He made the long journey to a local ophthalmology clinic run by The Himalayan Cataracts Project (HCP). The HCP was founded in 1995 by Dr. Sandak Ruit and Dr. Geoff Tabin. Because of the clinic and the surgeries performed there, 600,000 people in the developing world have had their sight restored during the last twenty years.

A cataract is a cloudy or opaque area in the normally transparent lens of the eye. The eye becomes progressively cloudy and grey, resulting in blurred vision, which eventually leads to a total loss of vision. There are 20 million people worldwide who are blind, and 85 percent of these people can be restored to perfect sight with a simple cataract surgery.

In undeveloped countries, the burden of blindness is much harsher than in the developed world. In Africa, the life expectancy for a blind person is one-third that of a sighted person. Blindness not only affects the blind person, but her family and the community. Often a child will be forced to drop out of school to care for a parent or grandparent who is blind, or an adult will have to leave the workforce to care for a blind relative. Blindness alters the lives of those close to them and can perpetuate generations of poverty and need. In Nepali villages, it is just a fact of life.

"You get old, your hair thins, your eyes turn grey, and then you die" one patient noted sadly.

When the HCP team began work two decades ago, one lens that was inserted into the eye of a cataract patient cost a blind person $200, which was more than the yearly earnings of most of the potential patients. Today, the lenses are produced locally in Nepalese manufacturing facilities and cost about $4 each to produce. The total cost of surgery in each eye costs just $25. The surgery takes only ten minutes per eye, and almost every patient sees perfectly the next day.

"That moment when a blind person realizes that they have had their sight restored, there is really nothing else like it. You really have to see it to understand it. It is pure joy," Dr. Tabin has said.

When the bandages come off and patients realize their vision is restored, they typically hoot and holler. They sing and dance. They weep with joy and drop to their knees. Some grandparents see their relatives for the first time in decades. Parents are finally able to lay eyes on their own children. When the patches come off and the eyes are opened, there is rarely a dry eye in the room. Restoring a blind person's sight also restores her or his sense of hope for the future. Sight gives people their lives back.

When they began the project, the HCP team had a backlog of 250,000 people that desperately needed surgical help. The mission of the HCP is to create a planet where nobody is needlessly blind. Although the two men initially performed all the surgeries themselves, they realized that training other doctors to perform the surgery was a much quicker way to cure people of this life-altering condition. There are now 550 HCP-trained ophthalmic personnel curing blind people across the globe.

Each day at an HCP clinic, over two-hundred people regain their site after the surgery, and 90 percent can pass a driver's eye test the day after surgery. Dr. Tabin noted, "From the moment I first saw the miracle of cataract surgery on a totally blind patient, I realized that there was nothing else in medicine as cost-effective that we can do to actually change someone's life instantaneously."

Dr. Ruit was born in a village in eastern Nepal. It was so remote that the nearest school was a week's walk away. There were no healthcare clinics, and Ruit's sister died of tuberculosis when he was seventeen. This experience led him to want to become a doctor. Ruit's sole mission is to bring eyesight back to anyone who needs it, regardless of his or her ability to pay. Ruit can perform dozens of flawless cataract operations at eye camps over the course of a twelve-hour day. Working tirelessly at the operating table, he says, "The surgical chair is the most comfortable place on Earth that I have."

After studying ophthalmology in India, Ruit returned to Nepal. He learned about a cataract micro-surgery technique using implanted intraocular lenses, and he wanted to utilize this technique to help the poorest of the poor. Ruit was the first Nepali doctor to perform cataract surgery with intraocular lens implants and the first to pioneer a method for delivering high-quality microsurgical procedures in geographically remote eye camps.

Dr. Geoff Tabin is cofounder and chairman of the Himalayan Cataract Project and a professor of ophthalmology and global medicine at Stanford University. Tabin is highly accomplished in the world of high-altitude mountain climbing, and this passion led him to his life's work. Dr. Tabin was the fourth person in the world to reach the tallest peak on each of the seven continents. After summiting Mt. Everest on one of his expeditions, he came across a Dutch team performing cataract surgery on a woman who had been needlessly blind for three years. It was then and there that he understood his life's calling.

The HCP team has vowed to work to eliminate all preventable and treatable blindness from the Himalayan region in their lifetime. It's a goal, which Tabin says is "more audacious than setting out to make the first assent of the East Face of Mount Everest." The Himalayan Cataract Project has expanded beyond the Himalayas to open clinics in Sub-Saharan Africa where HCP doctors deliver hundreds of blind people from the darkness every day.

Clearly these selfless doctors have combined their passion with a profound drive to make a difference in the lives of the less fortunate. Everyone has his or her own story, and every person has value. Most folks are not as blessed as you and I, and many people across the globe struggle on a daily basis just to survive.

Words to the Wise: If you are reading this book, then you are a very fortunate person. You can see. You have been taught to read. You have access to learning materials, a comfy chair, and shelter to read it in. You have the time to read, a full belly, and someone to call if you find yourself in need. Never forget that most people's skills and resources are far less abundant than yours, and always be generous with your time, money and passion.

You can learn more about this amazing team of people and the HCP at cureblindness.org.

CHAPTER 21

THE MONEY OR HER LIFE

"We want $150,000. Give us the money, or your aunt is going to die," the caller ominously said.

Haiti, and its capital Port-au-Prince, was besieged in 2004. Daily there were kidnappings with demands for large ransom payments. With between eight and ten people abducted every day, Haiti became known for having the highest kidnapping rate in the world. Although abductions for political purposes were usually quite violent, the kidnapping of ordinary citizens solely for the purpose of receiving ransom were usually very calm, routine, and businesslike. Men with black masks would pull up to a car or home and snatch a vulnerable victim, usually a woman, child, or elderly person. On this day, a prominent politician had been kidnapped. Her nephew had received the terrifying phone call and was panicked for his aunt's safety. Luckily for the victim, Chris Voss was on the case that day.

Chris Voss was the lead international kidnapping negotiator for the FBI in 2004 and was the foremost expert on the craft of negotiating with kidnappers. Voss was a member of the New York City Joint Terrorist Task Force from 1986 to 2000 and received hostage negotiator training at the Federal Bureau of Investigation's school in 1992. Voss spent twenty-four years working in the FBI Crisis Negotiation Unit and was the FBI's chief international hostage and kidnapping negotiator from 2003 to 2007.

In his 2016 book, *Never Split the Difference*, Voss tells the many harrowing tales of his intense career and makes many fascinating points about how best to negotiate whether with a hostage-taker, a boss or a new car salesman.

When the call came into the FBI that morning, the victim's nephew could only think of doing one thing: paying the ransom quickly and getting his aunt back alive. When thugs threaten to kill a relative unless they get their money, you don't really have any leverage, right? The FBI knew better, however. There is always leverage, and seasoned professionals know how to negotiate with hostage-takers to get innocent victims released unharmed.

According to Voss, the art of negotiation practiced by the FBI involves understanding the kidnapper, discovering what his real motives and desires are, and never giving an inch. A "split the difference" tactic of negotiation is never employed as the FBI either gets back the kidnapping victim alive or they do not. And giving in to a kidnapper with even 50 percent of what is demanded only reinforces the wisdom of grabbling someone off the street to make some easy money. The FBI takes a firm stand to work to achieve control of the tense situation and to never give in to the demands of a criminal.

In his book, Voss writes that the first rule of successful negotiation is realizing that there are no actual deadlines. A hostage-taker will always threaten a deadline for the payment of ransom, saying that if they don't receive it then something very specifically terrible will happen to the victim after that deadline. This is typically scary and unnerving. It is rarely true. Although our minds may adopt a reasonable fear of what will happen after that deadline passes, the result rarely comes to pass. Hostage deadlines are usually arbitrary, flexible, and hardly ever trigger the negative consequences that are promised. Patience in a negotiation is a formidable tool and weapon. Once the negotiator realizes that he has all the time in the world to conclude a stressful situation with a positive outcome that patience becomes a huge advantage for the negotiator. Voss notes that in all his years of working at the FBI and as a consultant to private companies, he has never seen the passage of an imagined deadline lead to negative repercussions. In his opinion, there is always more time to negotiate with a counterparty who wants something from you.

Second, the negotiator must ascertain what the true motives of their adversaries are. A few weeks into the Haitian kidnapping boom of 2004, Voss and his team noticed two things. First, Mondays seemed to be especially busy. It was as if the kidnappers had a work week and rose early on

Mondays ready to tackle that week's kidnapping toils. Second, they noted that the kidnappers seemed to be especially eager to make a deal as the weekend approached.

At first these factors did not make much sense to the FBI. But from the investigations of many kidnappings in Haiti that year, the kidnapper's true motives become obvious; the kidnappers were garden-variety thugs who wanted to get paid by Friday, so they could party through the weekend. Once the FBI understood the kidnapper's goals, the leverage was squarely on the side of the FBI. The negotiating team knew that if it let the pressure build by delaying its pressing for the hostage's release to Thursday, it would end up cutting a much better deal when the desperation of the kidnappers rose. And the FBI knew that having a fun party weekend in Haiti costs much less than $150,000, so the release of a hostage could come at a far cheaper price than was demanded. The agents also knew that oddly specific numbers usually seem much more reasoned and well thought out than big round numbers, such as $150,000.

Back in Haiti after learning that the ransom was just weekend party money, the FBI agents decided that they were willing to pay just $5,000, and they offered $3,000 as an initial bid. The weekend was approaching, so the kidnappers lowered their offer to $10,000. The FBI then put the nephew on the phone to make an offer with a strangely specific number, $4,751. The nephew stated that was the exact amount that could be raised from the family, and there was no more. The kidnappers declined the offer and then threatened to kill the aunt again. The nephew added a portable CD player to sweeten the offer. The kidnappers did not really want the CD player, but since it was offered, they felt that there was no more money to be had if the other side was now offering petty goods. The weekend was now imminent. The kidnappers grew desperate, and the deal was done. Six hours later, the family paid that sum and the aunt came home safely.

After working on more than 150 international hostage cases, Chris Voss retired from the FBI in 2007, and was given the Attorney General's Award for Excellence in Law Enforcement as well as the FBI Agents Association Award for Distinguished and Exemplary Service. Voss now runs the Black

Swan Group, which teaches proper negotiation skills to individuals, businesses, and governments.

<u>Words of the Wise:</u> Smart agents at the FBI know that negotiations are defined by a network of desires and needs that are hidden. They don't let themselves be fooled by what is on the surface. They know that splitting the difference is akin to agreeing to wear one black shoe and one brown shoe, which is a terrible compromise. Agreeing to meet halfway often leads to a bad deal for both sides of the negotiation.

CHAPTER 22

WHAT IS RISK?

Chris Hadfield is an amazing man and astronaut. Hadfield was the first Canadian astronaut to walk in space. He also flew on two space shuttle missions and served as commander of the International Space Station. With wisdom gained from his decades of high-risk service, he recently admitted something in a *Masterclass* lecture that was very interesting:

> The common portrayal of astronauts in the movies is that they are arrogant, thrill-seeking, fearless and swashbuckling. We are nothing like that. Astronauts don't like adrenaline running through their veins. They don't want to be thrilled by what's happening. They don't want to be overwhelmed by the journey. We want to be calm, cold, calculating, highly aware, and competent. We prepare for every possible situation so that we are not surprised by anything. We want to fly with people who have practiced endlessly and are prepared for any stress that may arise. You don't want someone up there who is reckless and supercharged, shouting, 'Hey, watch this!' Space flight is not supposed to be exciting. If it is thrilling, then you are doing it wrong. Landing is exciting as only then do you know if you were fully prepared, and successful in meeting every challenge.

This quote made me immediately think about investing and wealth management. While many new investors want their investments to be exciting to follow daily, a thoughtful, diversified long-term wealth management plan is not supposed to be a riveting creation. A well-diversified plan is not meant to provide daily entertainment. A wealth plan is not supposed to be exciting. Like space travel, a wealth plan is created and maintained by experienced folks who have seen it all, so they are fully capable and ready for any situation that occurs.

A wealth management plan is maintained by people who will not panic if the financial markets go haywire temporarily. A team that is calm and highly competent in a crisis. And people who can stay disciplined to the plan and can keep the investor focused on the future, no matter what happens in the markets in the short-term. Only upon "landing" in retirement or at some other predetermined goal does the investor feel the excitement of knowing that his or her financial future is well taken care of. If a portfolio or wealth plan is a thrill-ride every day, then you are doing it wrong.

Negativity always sounds more robust and reasoned than outright optimism does, and there will always be a morbid mob of pundits and prognosticators that fear each new all-time high and want you to feel that fear as well. However, there is nothing inherently dangerous about new market-high levels. Looking back at all new all-time market highs since 1928, the average return from a new market high over the next six months is a gain of 3.9 percent versus 3.6 percent on all other days. Over the next year from an all-time high, the market gained 7.8 percent versus 7.5 percent on all other days. Therefore, market performance is better than average following all-time highs, not worse. This fact is not mentioned in any the-sky-is-falling! articles, however.

Conversely, while a continually strong equity market does produce worry in some investors, in others it may create the opposite mindset. Over time, a well-diversified, long-term wealth plan has proven to be the best bet to weather any market cycle storm. However, strong stock market periods like this one may cause well-meaning, long-term investors to question the wisdom of investing in a wide variety of strategies and asset classes rather than just holding stocks.

The idea that all these strategies and asset classes do not move together in lockstep is exactly the point of developing a thoughtful long-term wealth management plan. It is what keeps investors from experiencing the full pain of an inevitable stock market correction when a recession does occur. And diversification is especially essential at times of market extremes. Many investors remember that the S&P 500 lost 39 percent of its value in 2008, but few people recall that the ten-year government bond *gained* 21 percent in 2008. While the ten-year bond may not be an exciting investment vehicle nor its yield a titillating topic at a cocktail party, a balanced portfolio of both stocks and bonds held up much better in that challenging market year of 2008 than holding stocks alone.

During happy times in the stock market, it can be easy for an intelligent investor to forget why he or she would want to continue to hold a well-diversified portfolio of strategies and asset classes. Much like a sports team or Broadway play, each contributor plays a different, but pivotal, role in the overall performance, and each plays that role only at the appropriate time. This diversification is essential in riding out the ebbs and flows of global economic cycles. With a diversified asset allocation plan, some asset classes or strategies will always seem boring or unessential at times. This is how we know that we are managing downside potential. This is how we know that our financial legacy is not at risk. And this is how we know that we are positioned to prosper through any inevitable market downturn or market chaos.

Hadfield was very good friends with the group of fellow astronauts who perished when the Space Shuttle Columbia broke up and crashed as it passed through Earth's atmosphere while attempting to land in February of 2003. He comforted many of the families that week, and in his own grief, he personally reflected on both the risks and rewards of space flight and his life's work. He said he came to a determination about the risks involved:

I always want to focus on the activities that I think are worth doing. What are the risks involved, and how can I address the actual risks so that I can achieve the things that are important to me. No astronaut launches for space with their fingers crossed. That is not how we deal with risk. We are ready to confront the risk head on. And we recognize that there is a difference between danger and fear. They are not synonymous. You can choose to be afraid, or you can choose not to. It's up to you. Nothing is scary, it is only how a person perceives something that makes it scary or not. The best antidote for fear is competence.

NASA lost Space Shuttle Challenger in 1986. It exploded shortly after launch. This was due to a faulty O-ring in one of its solid rocket boosters. It was the twenty-fifth launch of a space shuttle mission, so risk managers may have concluded that statistically there was now a 4 percent chance of a future disaster in these missions. However, NASA and its astronauts did not quit or give up on the program. They grieved, consoled each other, assessed what went wrong, and devised improvements to their training, specification guidelines, and equipment.

After recovering from the depths of that devastating loss of personnel, equipment and confidence, NASA was ready to launch the next space shuttle mission in September 1988, which was only thirty-two months after the most horrendous accident in its history. And NASA flew six more shuttle missions over the next year. The risk-taking men and women of NASA fear disaster just like the rest of us. But after a tragedy, they lick their wounds, learn from their mistakes, and get back out there to put their lives on the line again for the sake of discovery, knowledge, and human progress.

The world financial markets endured disaster in 2008-09 when a global financial crisis sent markets reeling, shaking the confidence of most investors. Unfortunately, many investors did not have the fortitude of NASA astronauts. In the spring of 2009, the stock market and the economy were at their bleakest, and many investors chose to sell their holdings because they could not take the perceived pain any longer. These short-sighted investors sold at the very low point of the crisis, and many were so scarred from this temporary crisis that they have remained in cash for the next decade. Their fear cost them the opportunity to participate in the longest bull market in history fueled by the strong economic recovery that inevitably followed the financial crisis. Day always follows night, and over the 242 years since the founding of the United States, our economy has always recovered from temporary financial crises.

<u>Words of the Wise:</u> After the Challenger disaster, somehow NASA was able to rise from a devastating loss and launch another shuttle in thirty-two months, even knowing the risks that were involved. Likewise, the United States economy has endured many shocks before, but has made it through every recession, depression, world war, energy crisis, and political scandal, and has then gone on to notch new highs 100 percent of the time. But investors tend to forget this stellar long-term record of eventual recovery. Many investor's perceptions of what constitutes risk are undeveloped and unsophisticated, and they unfortunately pay the price for this lack of understanding.

CHAPTER 23

THE NETWORK EFFECT

Google has it. Uber has it. Microsoft Windows has it. Apple iMessage has it. It's the very powerful business factor of the *network effect*.

A network effect is the positive contribution that an additional user of a good or service has on the value of that product to others. With a network effect, the value of a product or service increases greatly according to the number of other people who are using it.

A network effect is very different from *economies of scale*. Economies of scale typically helps the producer generate more profit but does little for the end-user besides getting the product at a lower price. The more products that a producer can make, the lower the production cost of each product. But the consumer does not get a better product. With the network effect, the more people that use the product or service then the more valuable the service becomes.

Whenever someone builds a product that works better when others are using it as well, the network effect has a chance to kick in. Microsoft Word has dominated the word-processing space over many decades because a user was better off using the same word processor as his workmates and friends, so he could exchange files. If users all used different word processing programs, then they could not collaborate and work together as easily.

A great example of the power of the network effect is the telephone. When Alexander Graham Bell invested the first telephone in 1876, he was the only person who had one. Therefore, while the phone was an amazing invention, it was useless because he could not call anyone. If he gave one to his friend and installed a line between the two, then that would expand the value of his phone in a huge way. When fifty people get a telephone, you have something. When everyone in town has one? Now we are talking about a powerful network effect.

The greater the number of users of a product, the greater the value of the product to each person. The second person to install a telephone may like the product, but it only becomes very useful if many others also install a phone. The fifty-first person does not intend to increase the value of the network when he buys a phone, but that is the outcome anyway.

In the early days of the telephone there were more than four-thousand local and regional telephone companies. You can see how that would be a problem though. If your neighbor had a different phone system, then you could not call her. This early lack of network effect lead to most of those phone service providers combining into what became the Bell System phone network. Now everyone could talk to each other. Isn't that nice? That was of course before cold-calling and spam-calls were invented, so folks were actually happy when the phone rang as they knew someone they liked was on the other end.

This network effect also applied to the value and usefulness of the internet. When four people had access to the internet, the network was not worth much. But when four billion people have access, you have a very valuable network indeed.

Uber is another example of the power of the network effect. Uber drivers want to be on a network with a lot of potential customers while customers want to have access to the most possible drivers so that they don't have to wait a long time for a ride. It is hard to tell what comes first, the tipping point of drivers or passengers, but when enough passengers downloaded the Uber app and enough people became drivers, then Uber became the ride of choice for a majority of customers. More customers caused more drivers to choose Uber, which caused more customers to sign up, and so on.

We see the effect today in online social networks. Sites like Facebook and Instagram increase in value to each current member as more users join the global group. There can also be a positive feedback loop as more people join a group, which causes others to join that same group. In the soft drink market, there can be two large players such as Coke and Pepsi because different consumers have different tastes. A consumer can drink a Coke one day and a Pepsi the next without affecting the quality of the experience, but there is no network effect in soft drink consumption because the use of one brand does not increase the value of that brand to other consumers.

However, there is a network effect if enough users use one product, such as Facebook. New social media users typically want to join the network with the most users so that they can go to only one site to reach all their friends and family. That large number of users then causes more people to join that site until one network has a huge monopoly of the market. Back in 2006, Facebook and Myspace were still small fledgling companies offering a similar product and network. However, as the growth of Facebook took off, enough people joined Facebook that it crowded out competitors from the network effect, which spelled doom for the formerly popular Myspace. Back then you could decide which social network platform to join. These days your rational choice is to join the network that your friends and family are on, so in effect your only choice is Facebook.

Even seemingly inferior versions of a product can end up dominating a market if they can achieve enough early-mover advantage to create a network effect. In the early 1990s, many users were convinced that Apple's operating system was superior to Microsoft's version. But Microsoft was adopted by enough personal computers to achieve a status as the standard computer operating system for businesses and consumers and has dominated as the standard system ever since.

There is a huge network effect in the internet search field. In the early days of the internet, there were many companies that marketed web-search products. But I would wager that you have never heard of Excite, WebCrawler, Lycos, or Infoseek. The word Google is now used as a verb and a noun. That's because enough web searchers used it. The network effect took hold. As more people and businesses used Google, the value of the network and its users increased exponentially. Once a consumer trusted that the most valuable and efficient internet search results came from Google, a consumer did not use any other product. That network effect spelled doom for Yahoo Search, Bing, and Ask Jeeves. Excite was the first mover with its search engine launched in 1993, but it lost the market to Google because Google harnessed the power of the network effect and dominated the space.

We can also see the power of the network effect today in Netflix content-streaming. More users subscribe to Netflix, which gives them more money to produce more content, which in turn attracts more subscribers and so on. If all your friends are talking about shows they binge-watch on Netflix, then do you really want to subscribe to an inferior different streaming service?

Words of the Wise: The opposite of a network effect happens when the value of a product is affected negatively by more use or copies of a product. The *Mona Lisa* is a very valuable piece of art. But if DaVinci had painted one hundred of them, each one would of course be less valuable than just the one copy sitting in The Louvre.

CHAPTER 24

PENALTY KICKS AND INVESTOR INACTION

A penalty kick in soccer is one of the most exciting and impactful shots in all of sports. It's goalie versus striker, one–on-one, winner-take-all. Taken from the penalty spot twelve yards away from the goal line, the penalty kick is a shot that can make an entire stadium of rowdy fans hold their breaths all at once, and given that a typical professional-level soccer game total score averages only 2.5 goals, the penalty kick can frequently decide the outcome of a soccer match.

In game theory, the penalty kick is classified as a "non-cooperative zero-sum game," meaning that neither participant can compel the other player to make a particular choice, and all gains by the goalkeeper (in the form of saved or missed penalty kicks) occur to the direct detriment of the striker, and vice versa. One player wins and the other player loses. There are no ties.

The success or failure of penalty kicks are not mere coin flips. The odds of success skews radically in the favor of the striker and against the goalie. With the penalty spot so close to the goal, after the kick the goalie has only hundredths of a second to locate the ball and stop the shot. With so little time to react, goalies attempt to guess what direction a striker will kick the ball and then typically commit to dive in one direction or the other to increase their chances of making a save. However, goalies are usually not successful in their attempts to make a save.

Ignacio Palacios-Huerta, a behavioral scientist at the London School of Economics, is the recognized expert in data collection and analysis in the science of penalty kicks. He manages a database of more than 11,000 penalty kick outcomes, and he has found that penalty kicks are successful for the ball striker 82 percent of the time. Shots that strikers make to their dominant side (a right-handed player is typically a stronger striker to the left side of the goal) convert to goals 82.7 percent of the time, and shots to the striker's non-dominant side convert to goals 81.1 percent of the time. These outcomes are so similar that there is little difference in success outcomes between a striker shooting to her dominant side or his weaker side.

Although Pacacios-Huerta's data analyzes shot success both when a player shoots to the left side of the goal and the right side of the goal, the more interesting data arises from when a player strikes the shot to the middle of the goal. Reviewing 440 penalty shots in his database from World Cup and European Championship tournaments from 1976 to 2016, he found that goalkeepers remained in the center of the goal (not diving right or left) only 3 percent of the time. Also, over this period strikers kicked their shots to the middle of the goal only 9 percent of the time. At 97 percent, the success rate for scoring a goal from a penalty kick to the upper center of the goal is materially higher than shooting at either the right side or the left side of the goal. So, the question must be asked: Why don't more strikers kick their shots to the center of the goal when success is almost always ensured?

The answer lies deep in the behavioral biases of the players. Both the goalie and the striker must not only gauge the chance of success from a particular choice, but also must weigh the consequences of failure of each of the choices. From the striker's standpoint, if they aim for either side of the goal and the shot is saved, then much of the credit will go to the goalkeeper for making a "great save." But if the striker aims the ball at the center of the goal and the goalie remains motionless and stops the shot, then the striker will look foolish to their teammates, coaches, and rowdy fans. Strikers, therefore, have a bias toward action, any action except the perceived inaction of shooting straight ahead. If strikers are going to fail, then they at least want to fail in an acceptable way.

From goalies' perspectives, if they dive left or right, then at least they are making a strong attempt to stop a shot that had a high chance of getting by them anyway. They will feel less fault and culpability for the resulting goal.

However, if goalies simply stand in place and the ball finds the back of the net on the right or left side, then they may be seen as "not even trying" and may appear and feel foolish in the minds of those who would judge them. The goalies have a bias toward action and want to give at least the appearance of effort, and any action is seen as better than the inaction of standing in place. The behavioral desire to fail for the right reasons overwhelms each player's own self-interest to maximize the odds of his or her own success.

We have seen examples of this desire to fail for the right reasons all through business history as well. Throughout the twentieth century, a common expression was, "You will never get fired for choosing IBM." That meant business executives with a choice of firms for providing computer services would minimize their own responsibilities for failure of a project if they chose the industry standard. Although IBM may not have had the superior product or service, IBM was seen as the only safe bet. When a project managers were tasked with choosing the best piece of software or consultancy they could for a certain project, they frequently chose IBM to shield themselves from repercussions if anything had gone wrong. That's because IBM had the strongest perceived reputation for not allowing projects to fail. The executives concluded that if they were going to fail, then they would at least do it in the most acceptable manner.

This desire to fail for the right reasons is often seen in investor behavior and wealth management as well. Looking at S&P 500 returns since World War II, the index shows a positive performance in 54 percent of all individual trading days. So, on a short-term basis, an investor's success closely resembles a coin flip. However, the longer the timeframe, the higher the odds are of success. Over a calendar quarter, investors have a 69 percent chance of gaining a positive return. Over a year, they have an 82 percent chance of achieving a positive return. Over five years, 88 percent. Over ten years, 95 percent. And over any twenty-year period, S&P 500 investors have a 100 percent chance of gaining a positive return.

With such a high chance of equity market success and positive returns over longer periods of time, why do investors feel the need to worry about daily economic and market headlines, attempting to time the market by holding large cash balances or trade in and out of asset classes based on gut feel? The answer is the same behavioral bias toward action that is seen in soccer players attempting to be successful in penalty kicks. When faced with stress, humans tend to prefer action over inaction. Like soccer players, investors feel the need to take perceived control of a situation. They don't want to standby, passively ceding control to market forces. While both soccer players and stock market investors know that it is in their best interests to play the highest odds possible, humans still favor action over inaction. Even after millions of years of human evolution, people still have a very hard time remaining motionless in a time of stress whether on a soccer field or in a stock market correction.

As humans, we want to feel that we are in control over our own destiny and will feel more foolish if we take no action and harm befalls us than if we make concrete decisions to take action and the same misfortune comes to pass. Although penalty-kick goals are winner-take-all and there are no do-overs, with stock market investing there is always another day, quarter or year to overcome the temporary misfortune of a negative return. Long-term success can be achieved if investors do not succumb to making emotional short-term decisions that damage the long-term chance of success of their investment goals.

Words of the Wise: In both soccer and investing, inaction with the odds on your side has proven to be the best route to success. With a high chance of investor success over a long period of time, the best action in times of market volatility or correction is usually no action at all.

CHAPTER 25

BOUNCE BACK

The greatest glory in living lies not in never falling, but in rising every time we fall.

—*Nelson Mandela*

Diane Hendricks has made a habit of bouncing back from adversity. She was once a seventeen-year-old single mother in a small Midwestern town. In 2018, she was named by *Forbes Magazine* as America's richest self-made woman. That's because of her net worth of more than $6.8 billion. And I bet you have never even heard of her.

Diane Hendricks grew up on a dairy farm in rural Wisconsin. She was one of nine daughters and loved living on a farm, but she always dreamed of wearing a suit and running a business. When she was seventeen, she had a child with her "first love." This changed her life significantly. She did what her parents thought was the right thing to do and married her child's father. Due to her teen pregnancy, she was unable to continue in her high school class and was forced to complete her studies at home to earn her high school diploma.

To earn money and make ends meet, she got a job working on an assembly line at Parker Pen Company. She couldn't stand working in a factory and left after three months to sell new home construction. She knew she needed to acquire the skills to support herself on her own because she didn't think her marriage would last. She was correct, and Diane filed for divorce a week after her twenty-first birthday. Although she knew that she could raise her son on her own, her life looked bleak and uncertain.

Soon she met Ken Hendricks, a roofing contractor, and the pair began buying older, inexpensive houses in town, renovating them, and then selling them or renting them out. Within three years, they had bought and renovated a hundred homes in the Beloit, Wisconsin area. To keep costs low, the partners performed most of the renovation work themselves with just the help of Ken's father. Diane painted about two hundred units herself over their formative business years. The duo married in 1975.

After their wedding, Ken wanted to get into the roofing distribution business. They bought three small roofing stores in Illinois and Michigan during the depths of an economic recession. Those purchases were the beginning of ABC Supply Inc. which now has more than 350 locations and employs over five-thousand employees nationwide.

After many years of hard work building a very valuable company, tragedy struck. While inspecting the roof of his own house, Ken fell through the roof. He died from his injuries shortly after Christmas in 2007. Diane had not prepared for a future without her husband, but she needed to bounce back again through the intense pain of losing a treasured spouse. The Hendricks family owned thirty companies in the businesses of manufacturing, transportation, logistics, and insurance. Diane knew that the family of companies was their life's work and that she had to carry on through her grief for the sake of her husband's memory.

After her husband's death, Diane took control of the companies' operations. She has grown what was once a modest shingle-supply company into the largest roofing distributor in the United States. She completed many bold acquisitions of industry competitors, including the 2016 purchase of L&W Supply for $670 million. That purchase catapulted the company from a $3 billion revenue business at the time of Ken's death into a $9 billion business today.

Diane has also been on a crusade of sorts to give back to her little corner of the world, Beloit, Wisconsin. Located on the border of Wisconsin and Illinois, about a ninety-minute drive from Milwaukee, Beloit had fallen on hard times over the years as many of the manufacturing companies that were the employee lifeblood of Beloit had either gone out of business or moved away.

Diane set about to revitalize her once-proud town, and bought the local country club, shopping mall, the city's historic library, and many abandoned buildings and other properties with the goal of revitalizing them and bringing new businesses to the town. She even founded and ran the Beloit International Film Festival, which has attracted large crowds and celebrities to Wisconsin every January.

Although she and her husband excelled at renovating dilapidated houses, making over a whole town will be a major job even for someone with Diane's work ethic and financial resources. But if anyone can tackle a task that large and succeed, it is Diane Hendricks.

Words of the Wise: Diane Hendricks has demonstrated to the world that setbacks are not certain. Failure is not final. And through hard work and determination, anyone with grit and perseverance can make it through dark times and into the light on the other side.

CHAPTER 26

What is a Credit Rating?

Credit is a contractual agreement between a borrower and a lender. The borrower receives something of value now, usually money, and agrees to repay the lender at some date in the future. The borrower usually agrees to pay interest to the lender for the use of that money over the specific period.

The use of credit to purchase something should only be undertaken if the borrower can afford to make periodic payments of principal and interest to the lender, and if the borrower can pay back the whole debt when it comes due. However, a consumer's ability to get credit and having a good credit score is extremely important in today's society even if the credit is never used.

If you apply for a job, then your perspective employer may check your credit rating to assess your character related to your demonstrated responsibility in paying back your debts. If you move to a new house and apply to have the electricity and water turned on, then the utility companies may access your credit profile to determine if they need to ask for a large deposit for future payments. Or if you apply for a home mortgage loan or an auto loan, then the lenders will review your credit history to help decide whether to loan you money for the purchase, and at what interest rate they will charge for that loan.

Usually the lower your credit score, the higher the rate of interest that you will pay for borrowing money. A weak credit history demonstrates that the risk of lending money to you is much higher than the average borrower. Likewise, the higher your credit rating, the more favorable borrowing terms you will receive. Credit scores are the main factor used by potential lenders and creditors, such as banks, credit card companies or car dealerships as one factor to review when deciding whether to offer you credit, like a loan or credit card.

A *FICO score* is your credit score. Your credit score is a three-digit number ranging from 300 to 850, and this number reflects your history of paying back your debts on time. A borrower wants this score to be as high has possible. Credit scores are calculated using information in your credit report. That includes your payment history, the amount of debt a borrower has already, and the length of your credit history.

Credit scores from 580 to 669 are generally considered fair; 700 to 749 is considered good; and 750 and up is considered an excellent credit score. Higher credit scores mean that the potential borrower has demonstrated responsible credit behavior in the past, which may make potential lenders and creditors more confident when evaluating a request for credit.

Lenders generally see those with credit scores 670 and up as acceptable or low-risk borrowers. Those with credit scores from 580 to 669 are "subprime borrowers," meaning they may find it more difficult to qualify for better loan terms or will pay a much higher interest rate if the loan is approved. Those with lower scores, under 580, fall into the "poor" credit range and may have difficulty getting credit or qualifying for better loan terms.

Words of the Wise: Given the importance of a good credit score, a consumer must keep a very vigilant watch over their credit history and credit score as this history can make one's financial life much easier or much more expensive. Consumers can access a free copy of their credit report every year by using the websites of the three major credit history companies, Experian, Transunion and Equifax. Reviewing your credit report at least once a year is a great idea, to review where you stand, to look for errors to be corrected, and to look for ways to improve a credit rating score.

CHAPTER 27

WHERE THE STREETS HAVE NO NUMBERS

10 Downing Street. 1600 Pennsylvania Avenue. 221B Baker Street. 704 Hauser Street. Some street addresses are famous, but most are not memorable. While street addresses are a common fact of life in our world today, it was not always so until recent centuries.

Between 1715 and 1789, The Age of Enlightenment in Europe brought to society a new focus on science and ideas. These ideas decreased the power of the church and the authority of the established monarchies and paved the way for the political revolutions of the eighteenth and nineteenth centuries. The Enlightenment included a new range of ideas centered on reason as the primary source of authority and came to advance ideals like liberty, progress, tolerance, and constitutional government. These new ideas eventually led to the French Revolution in 1789.

As Anton Tantner of the University of Vienna wrote in his exhaustive study of this odd part of world history, *House Numbers: Pictures of a Forgotten History*, the Enlightenment brought many advances to Europe, but none were as important as the implementation of street names and house numbers. House numbers were not always common or inevitable. They were a needed invention and their rollout caught on quickly but with great controversy. Street numbers were not in use until the 1700s. Prior to then, the small populations of towns and the low mobility of most citizens meant that people lived in one house for a very long time, and everyone else in town knew where they lived. Streets sometimes had a name, but houses were not numbered. And it made for a very confusing situation for visitors trying to find a friend or emergency workers attempting to give aid to the stricken.

Often a house was named for its owner and if he moved, then it took on the name of the new owner. Many houses took the same popular name, which led to obvious confusion. For instance, in 1700s Vienna there were six houses in the city with the name *The Golden Eagle*, and twenty-three more in the suburbs.

Lack of house numbers also led to corruption at the local government level. When a state government worker needed to locate a citizen in a town, he frequently had to rely on the local lords for information. This privileged information cost money, and the lords profited from the information they could provide to outsiders.

The delivery of mail was not a reason for designating houses with numbers. The local postmen knew which citizens lived where. Street numbers were first introduced by local or state governments for the purposes of keeping track of citizens for conscription as soldiers in wartime, and for the payment and collection of taxes.

The purpose of the early idea for house numbering was not to provide the houses with an address; it was to keep track of the city's wealth. If the city officials did not know who lived in a house, then they could not know how much wealth resided at that address. Taxing citizens was difficult. Numbering began in the suburbs of Paris in 1724, Prussia in 1737, Madrid in 1750, and London in 1762. By the end of the 1700s, most homes in Europe were now adorned with house numbers.

While house numbering seems like a simple and logical idea now, the initiation of street numbers led to controversy from all ranks of society. Advocates for the lower classes viewed house numbers as "a symbol of the hand of the ruler determinedly taking possession of the private individual." The elites in society did not care for the numbering of houses either, feeling that they did not approve of the egalitarian nature of numbers. To the wealthy, the idea meant that wealthy houses were numbered similarly as the humble commoner dwellings of society. But after house numbering, cities were now easier to navigate, and people were easier to find. A peasant's home was numbered in the same way as an aristocrat's.

Street numbers were first initiated with the lowest number on the first house on the left side of a street, continuing all the way down that side and then switching sides at the end of the street, then the numbers continued higher coming back on the other side. Therefore, the lowest number on a street was directly across from the highest number. This style of numbering led to inevitable confusion. The system of odd-numbered houses on one side of the street and even-numbered houses on the other side was first instituted in Paris in 1805.

The controversy and disagreement regarding street names and house numbers continues to this day, and an address is now an essential part of proving one's identity. In today's society, if a citizen wants to register for school, turn on electric service, open a bank account, or vote in elections, then she is required to provide a street address.

In 2018, the United States Supreme Court heard a case involving Native Americans in North Dakota and their claim of voter disenfranchisement due to voter registration requirements. North Dakotans are not allowed to vote unless they can provide identification that shows their name, birth date, and residential address. Many people on Native American reservations don't have residential addresses. These citizens use post office boxes to receive their mail, but a P.O. box is not sufficient proof of residence to vote in North Dakota. The Supreme Court upheld the law requiring an address to vote, so eighteen-thousand people in North Dakota who do not have a street address are not be able to vote.

Words of the Wise: While the Age of Enlightenment brought a sense of reason and equality to the world with street names and house numbers, the now near-universal use may cause discrimination for those without street addresses. In fact, some charities have a stated mission to travel to disadvantaged parts of the world like the slums of Calcutta, West Virginia, and South Africa to work with local governments to assign street names and house numbers to the modest homes of the poor. A street address can make the difference between life and death, not only in voting in elections and receiving government aid, but in the ability of first responders to find someone who calls 911 before they die.

CHAPTER 28

WHAT IS A SHORT SELLER?

An old man on his way home from work received a call from his wife who said, "Honey, please be careful driving. I just saw a news report that said there is someone driving the wrong way down the highway."

The husband replied "Oh sweetie, you don't know the half of it! There are hundreds of them!"

We have discussed what it means to buy a stock and own a stock. In market speak, buying a stock is called *going long* and owning a stock is called *being long* the stock. But you may have also heard the term *being short* stock, *selling short*, or being a *short seller* of shares. The short position is exactly the opposite of being long. You are betting that the price of the shares will fall rather than increase in value. Investors may make this negative bet against a stock if they do not like the company or its products, if they believe the company's management or its financial statements are suspect, or if they feel that a company's large debt load may hurt the company's long-term prospects. There are many reasons an investor may want to bet against a company's shares, but only one good way to do it: by *shorting* the stock.

What does it mean to short a stock? An investor will borrow stock from someone else and sell the shares into the market. He will later buy back shares in the market, hopefully at a lower price than he sold them for initially. That's how he will replace the shares he borrowed and make a profit from the decline in the stock price.

As an example, let's say a teenager's parents went out of town for the weekend on Friday, and left their responsible son at home with Dad's new car. Later that day, the doorbell rings.

At the door is a man who says, "Sorry to bother you, but I just love that Mercedes in the driveway, and I must buy it from you."

The son thinks about the idea and replies, "Okay, fine. But I want $50,000."

"Done" says the man, who immediately hands the cash to the boy, and drives off in the car.

The boy has sold something that he does not own, so he is now *short* one Mercedes. The industrious teen now *really* needs to find an exact replica of his dad's car to replace it with, and he needs to do it by Sunday at 6:00 P.M. when his dad returns home. The teen searches all day Saturday, and locates the exact same model, and finds it a great price of $40,000. The teen buys the car, parks it in the driveway, and his dad is never the wiser. Since he bought the car for $40,000 and sold it for $50,000, the teen has profited by $10,000. He just did it in the reverse order of a typical purchase-and-sale transaction.

In the stock-investing world, a short investor will need to work with a brokerage firm to borrow shares that he does not own so that he may sell them short. When the brokerage firm locates shares, the investor will borrow the shares and sell them in the market. He is now short those shares and will have to buy the exact number of shares back at some point in the future. If he sells the shares for $50 a share, then he will need to buy back shares later at a price less than $50 to make a profit. The problem for the investor arises if the price of the shares increases. If the price of the shares rise to $60 a share, then the investor now has potential losses of $10 a share. If the investor gets nervous and chooses to close out his position in the short at $60 a share, then he will have to pay $10 more a share than he sold the stock for initially. The stock price could even rise to $100 or $150 or higher. The investor would then lose a lot of money if he were forced to buy the stock at $100 after initially selling it for only $50. He would need to make up the loss by adding more money to his brokerage account.

A situation called a *short squeeze* is also a possible danger in shorting a stock. Going back to our example, let's say the teen was unable to find an exact copy of his dad's car at a reasonable price. And that three other neighborhood teens had also sold their dads' cars short that weekend. It is now Sunday at 3:00 P.M. and all the boys start panicking. With such high demand for the same car, the price of the only cars available rise to $75,000 each. There are no other options as the dads are headed home soon. Our original teen is forced to borrow $25,000 from a friend. He combines that money with the $50,000 that he received on Friday so that he can buy the replacement car. Selling his dad's car short was a terrible idea, the teen concludes.

Words of the Wise: For most investors, selling stock short is a bad idea. Buying stock to hold for the long-term is investing, but selling stock short that you may be forced to pay a much higher price for later on to replace the borrowed shares is gambling and is very risky. Historically, stock prices usually rise over time, so it is best to keep to the long side of the market. An investor does not want to be driving on the wrong side of the road on a one-way street.

CHAPTER 29

WHY FREE TRADE MAKES THE WORLD GO 'ROUND

"It is a curious thing about the language used in a trade war. Tariffs are frequently referred to as protectionist measures. Tariffs do in fact offer protection as they protect consumers from low prices."

—Economist Milton Friedman

A flour salesman walked into a bakery one day and said to the owner, "Hello sir, my company produces the best flour in the world. We produce it with raw materials from my country so that your own wheat stores are not depleted. We mill it in our factories so that your air is not polluted. My workers grind it and pack it so that your citizens can be employed in higher-value work. We ship it to you on our ships so that your ships are free for other purposes. Lastly, I want to sell my product to you for below the cost at which you could produce it yourself. Would you like to buy some?"

The bakery owner thought for a minute and replied, "Fine, as long as I can pay you in store credit only."

The flour salesman readily agreed, and both men walked away happy.

Does this sound like a good deal for the salesman or his company? It certainly does not. Yet this is exactly the good deal that the United States receives when we run a *trade deficit,* or what may be more accurately called a *goods surplus* if you are transacting on the side of the United States While all the talk these days seems to be around the subject that running a trade deficit is detrimental to the United States and its workers, there are many arguments that have been made over the last few hundred years that argue against the idea of trade protection.

The *store credit* idea is a very powerful part of the deal above, and one that is rarely thought of as a significant benefit to the buyer of foreign goods. When we purchase foreign-made goods, we purchase them with dollars. What then happens to those dollars? They can be spent immediately in the United States to purchase other goods, or they can be shipped back to the goods-producing country. They may even be used to purchase goods in other countries.

Even if the dollars bounce around the world economy for a while, they will eventually find their way back to the United States to purchase our goods and services. This is the only country where they have purchasing value, so the store credit that we used to buy goods from other countries will eventually be redeemed at our "store." The dollars may even be used to purchase goods made from the cheap raw materials that were sold to us below cost in the first place.

Then why have the perceived benefits of tariffs and protectionist trade policy continually endured over the preceding many centuries? It's because the benefits of tariffs are small but visible while the detriments and costs are large but invisible. If we protect our domestic steel industry, then a small group of steelworkers may not lose their jobs, and steelworkers are an identifiable voting bloc that can show up at the polls. The much larger group of "consumers who will pay an extra ten dollars per washing machine due to tariffs" is not a distinct voting bloc. This group is not identifiable, and no one will march on Washington, D.C. to get their ten dollars back.

A small group with strong incentives can usually outmaneuver a large group with small incentives, at least in the short term. However, the essence of protectionist tariffs is that they benefit a small group of workers at the expense of a large group of consumers. The essence of free trade is that it benefits a large group of consumers at the expense of a small group of workers.

Some investors worry about the harmful effects of a trade deficit as well. A *budget deficit* where a government spends more than it receives in taxes can be a legitimate problem for the health and credit rating of the country in the long run. Remember, a trade deficit is not necessarily a bad thing and does not say much about either country's economic strength or its future economic well-being.

For example, if your neighbor owns a grocery store and you own a shoe store, and you spend $200 a month at his store and he spends only $50 at your store, then that is a trade deficit and may seem unfair to you. However, it says nothing about the health or future viability of his business or yours. You can both thrive if you offer value to enough other customers by focusing on what you do well and earning profits that exceed costs.

<u>Words of the Wise:</u> The nature of effective global trade revolves around specialization where a country focuses on the production of a limited scope of goods to gain greater efficiency. Many countries specialize in producing the goods and services that are native to their parts of the world, and they trade for other goods and services that they do not or cannot produce. This specialization is the basis of global trade as few countries have enough production capacity to be completely self-sustaining.

CHAPTER 30

What is Compounding?

During the frequent conversation between a space shuttle crew and mission control in a space shuttle launch sequence, you would typically hear a command from the flight control center of "Houston. Go at throttle up." This happens about one minute after the shuttle leaves the launch pad. Sadly, although the acceleration was unrelated to the subsequent explosion, this command was the last verbal communication between mission control and the crew of the Space Shuttle Challenger before it exploded in a ball of fire in January of 1986. The vessel was at about 48,000 feet of altitude when that command came.

It would seem as if the rocket would be traveling at top speed already as it streaks away from Earth and would not need an additional boost of power. However, while the rocket is gaining altitude at a tremendous velocity, aerodynamic forces keep it from travelling at full speed until the rocket rises to an altitude with much thinner air. Gaining altitude at full speed in the thick air near sea level would put too much pressure and aerodynamic drag on the rocket and would tear it apart. It would be like slamming into a brick wall. Hence the call for "go at throttle up" when the ship arrives at a safe altitude with thinner air.

The ship would then accelerate to its maximum velocity to slip the surly bonds of gravity and continue on its journey to space. In the language of astrophysics, a Max-Q point is the altitude level where the increasing speed of the rocket is outweighed by the decreasing density of the atmosphere as the rocket climbs higher, and the air pressure and aerodynamic danger decreases from that point on. It is then safe and easy to shoot higher on its mission to space.

The investment equivalent to throttle up is the power of compounding and the benefits of compound interest. In simple terms, *compound interest* means that an investor begins to earn interest income on his interest income, resulting in his money growing at an ever-accelerating rate. Like a rocket after launch, in the initial years of an investment, the account balance struggles to gain much traction, but later on these small gains become large gains.

For instance, if you invested $1,000 and earn a 10 percent interest rate, then at the end of year-one you have $1,100. If you then earn 10 percent of interest on that new higher total, then you end up with $1,210 at the end of the second year. Not only does your initial investment earn interest, but the interest that you have earned and left in the account also then earns interest. At the end of the fifth year, you will have $1,611. At the end of the tenth year, you will have $2,594, and at the end of the twentieth the amount will have grown to $6,757.

The longer the time frame that you can compound a sum, the greater the effects of compounding. A rocket ship finds it easier to gain altitude the higher the ship goes. That's because the air is thinner and there is less resistance. Similarly, the power of compounding makes it far easier to earn an additional dollar the larger the account balance and the longer the time frame for compounding.

Starting the compounding journey while young is especially powerful. For example, let's look at three investors. Troy saved $1,000 per month from the time he turned twenty-five until he turned thirty-five. At that point, he stopped saving but left his money in his investment account where it continued to grow at a seven percent rate until he retired at sixty-five.

Carla went to medical school and didn't start saving until age thirty-five. She put away $1,000 per month from her thirty-fifth birthday until she turned forty-five. She also then stopped saving but left the balance in her investment account where it continued to compound at a rate of seven percent until she was sixty-five.

Harry did not know about the power of compounding and didn't get around to investing until age forty-five. Still, he invested $1,000 per month for ten years, and stopped saving at age fifty-five. He also left his money to accrue at a seven percent rate until his sixty-fifth birthday. Troy, Carla and Harry each saved the same amount, $120,000, over a ten-year period. But due to the power of compounding, their ending balances were dramatically different.

Account balance at age 65:

Troy: $1,125,365

Carla: $572,079

Harry: $290,816

Words of the Wise: There is no brilliance in harnessing the power of compound interest to grow wealth over time. An investor simply needs patience and a long-time frame, and the power will work by itself. Start early. Invest often. Don't touch the balance. And magic will happen to your small investment over time.

CHAPTER 31

TIME IS WORTH MORE THAN MONEY

Here is a fascinating choice involving the true value of money and large wealth versus the value of time.

Would you trade places with Warren Buffett if you were offered every dollar of Warren Buffett's fortune right now?

You may initially conclude that of course you would! But imagine having Buffett's wealth, fame, and status as the greatest investor on Earth. You can go anywhere you please, meet anyone you want, and buy anything that can be sold.

However, you're now eighty-nine years old. You are far past your life expectancy, and you could "move on" any day. Would you still make that switch? I would not, under those conditions, and most people would not either, even considering his vast wealth.

Although most Americans are constantly worried about the pressures and challenges of producing, growing, and maintaining their incomes and piles of wealth, this choice lays bare what we all may value most, which is time. The time to experience new things, time with family, time to grow an interesting career, time to meet new friends and time to travel the world. Time seems to be what most folks value most when given the choice.

And likewise, if you gave Warren Buffett the choice to stay where he is now or immediately become eighteen again but be completely broke? What choice do you think he would make? I think he would choose to get his seventy years back with the opportunity to start his wealth-building journey all over again. It may be a comfort to the average broke eighteen-year-old that if given the choice, Warren Buffett would trade places with him.

Bronnie Ware is an Australian nurse who spent several years caring for patients in the last twelve weeks of their lives. She recorded her patients' dying thoughts, wishes, and regrets and put her observations into a book called *The Top Five Regrets of the Dying*. Ware noted that most regrets at life's end centered around five thoughts:

> *I wish I'd had the courage to live a life true to myself, not the life others expected of me.*
> *I wish I hadn't worked so hard*
> *I wish I'd had the courage to express my feelings.*
> *I wish I had stayed in touch with my friends.*
> *I wish that I had let myself be happier.*

Words of the Wise: As an old person lays dying, the wish is very rarely for more money but for more time. Although you are young now and might feel like you have all the time in the world left, what will you set out to achieve or change before you die?

CHAPTER 32

THREE POWERFUL PARTNERS

When thinking about retirement planning, it can be a daunting task for a young person to sacrifice earnings now to be able to be live a comfortable and stress-free financial life forty years from now. It may feel like a dollar saved and invested now will not make much of a difference in the future as the contributions are so small. So what is the point? As a young professional just starting out, you may feel small, alone, and insecure about saving and planning for the future. However, you are absolutely not alone, and you do not need to work toward this goal by yourself. You have two very powerful and helpful partners in growing wealth over time, so three members of your team can attack the challenge instead of just one.

I entered my company's 401(k) plan in 1992, at age twenty-five. I am now fifty-two years old and looking back over the past twenty-seven years of investing there have been many market cycles, recessions, bull markets, a financial crisis, and countless periods of market volatility. However, as I look at my 401(k) account balance today, I am pleased that it has grown into a sum that is well on its way to providing a good nest egg and potential for strong income generation at retirement. But more importantly, I notice how it grew over time, and what help I had along the way. Looking at the sources of the total account now, one-third of the balance came from my own paycheck contributions over the years, one-third came from my employer match and profit-sharing contributions, and one-third came from investment market gains over this long period of time.

It is clear that combining my own contributions, doubled by an employer contribution match, and investing in stocks over a long period of time is a really powerful combination in meeting one's long-term retirement planning goals. Market gains from being consistently invested in equities over a long period of time, combined with employer contributions, is a very strong lever than can lift far more load than my contributions could alone.

A recent report stated that the preferred 401(k) investment vehicle for millennials is cash. While keeping retirement savings in cash may seem like a safe choice, inflation has averaged 2.9 percent over the last forty years, so inflation diminishes any return that comes from holding cash. And a cash investor is forgoing the two strongest wealth accumulation weapons in a young person's arsenal: time and the power of compounding. The United States economy has grown steadily for the last 225 years, and it has had only occasional and brief periods of slowdown. Not betting on this strong economic horse to help grow wealth over time is a terrible mistake.

I have also considered what I did right over the years, and what I did wrong:

Good moves:

1) I have been consistently invested in a diversified portfolio of equity strategies and have invested new contributions during good times and bad.

2) I have not tried to time the market based on gut feelings. The S&P 500 has risen in 73 percent of the last hundred calendar years, and market returns have bested the inflation rate in 80 percent of those years, so attempting to beat the odds by market timing is not a good bet to make.

3) I did not borrow from the account or take distributions. Any time that your money is not working in the account for your benefit is a lost opportunity for growth.

Bad moves:

1) I bought individual stocks at times, which is not a productive focus for a long-term retirement planning account. In February of 2000, I bought a small tech stock at the peak of the dot-com craze that then lost most of its value over the next year. I learned a

great lesson however, and I kept the shares in the account for the next fifteen years at its tiny market value as a constant reminder that buying individual stocks in a retirement account is a bad idea. Looking back, that small loss paid off for the account over the years as it kept my investment choices and long-term focus on the straight and narrow.

Words of the Wise: With the very long timeframe that is the nature of a 401(k) plan account, it is clear that you can survive some small mistakes and still meet your long-term goals. If you consistently invest for the future and let your two powerful partners help do the heavy lifting, then you will be successful in meeting your goals on your retirement planning journey.

CHAPTER 33

WHAT IS INFLATION?

"Once an independent central bank does not simply tolerate a low level of inflation as consistent with 'stability,' but invokes inflation as a policy, it becomes very difficult to eliminate."

—Former Federal Reserve Chairman Paul Volcker,
September 2011

Inflation is the rate at which the general level of prices for goods and services is rising and the purchasing power of the currency is falling. Central banks such as the United States Federal Reserve attempt to limit inflation to keep the economy running smoothly. Due to inflation, the purchasing power of a unit of currency falls. For example, if the inflation rate is 2 percent, then a burger that costs $1 this year will cost $1.02 next year. When goods and services require more money to purchase over time, the implicit value of that currency falls.

A small amount of inflation is needed and is not particularly harmful as not only the level of prices increases, but wage levels also rise. Everyone wants a raise after all, and business owners want the price of their products to increase over time, so a small amount of inflation is tolerated. But major economic harm can occur when the rate of inflation rises too much over time.

Investors under forty must wonder why there is so much consternation about the possibility of a rise in inflation and its harmful effects on the economy. After all, inflation has averaged a benign level of 2.9 percent over the last forty years and has averaged 3.1 percent over the last ninety years. However, older market participants still remember the period of 1968-1981 when inflation raged, peaking at 13.3 percent in 1981. Runaway inflation in that era caused long periods of sluggish economic growth and high unemployment.

The Great Inflation was the defining macroeconomic event of the second half of the last century. Over the nearly two decades that it lasted, the global monetary system established after World War II was abandoned. The result was four economic recessions, two severe energy shortages, and the unprecedented peacetime implementation of wage and price controls. According to prominent economist Jeremy Siegel it was, "The greatest failure of American macroeconomic policy in the postwar period."

The story began after World War II when the Employment Act of 1946 was passed. Policymakers were still scarred by the rampant unemployment of the Great Depression in the 1930s, so this act put the federal government's focus squarely on employment growth. This focus morphed into a new economic theory in which employment growth could be "bought" with higher inflation, therefore inflation was allowed to rise. Eventually, inflation (which in the past was considered only a benign nuisance) was used as a tool to grow the number of jobs and reduce unemployment.

Over time, higher inflation became a self-fulfilling prophecy as labor unions and businesses expected higher inflation in the future and demanded higher wages and product prices immediately. The hoped for "stable tradeoff" between employment and higher inflation failed on both counts as by the summer of 1980 inflation was running near 14.5 percent and unemployment was near 8 percent.

The inflation that caused the lost decade only started to improve after the passage of the Humphrey Hawkins Act in 1978. The act instituted the federal government's dual mandate of a laser focus on full employment with price stability. This policy has been followed ever since. For forty years, this focus on a low and stable inflation rate has generated steady and impressive results, and it even may seem as if the government has been able to kill rampant inflation for good. However, even after this long period of price stability, many investors and economists still bear the scars of the 1970's, so will probably always worry about inflation's return.

If the Great Inflation was a consequence of a great failure of American macroeconomic policy, then the resulting thirty-eight-year long period of low inflation should be considered a triumph. In addition to a vigilant focus by the government on stable price levels, things may have changed in the economy from forty years ago that will prevent inflation spikes as well.

Employees have less wage leverage than they used to enjoy. The percentage of workers belonging to a labor union in the United States peaked in 1954 at almost 35 percent of the workforce, and the total number of union members peaked in 1979 at an estimated 21.0 million. Although the membership of public sector unions continues to grow steadily with active government position hiring, labor union membership in private industry has declined steadily since then to only 14.1 million which is a much smaller percentage of our growing economy than ever before.

The business marketplace is much more global than it used to be. Expansion of manufacturing production to the global marketplace and emerging economies means workers are in competition with a global labor pool. Rising labor costs in our country may mean a shift of production to lower-cost countries. Businesses are not confined to higher costs in the United States these days and will move businesses to where profit margins are the greatest.

The rise of technology and automated manufacturing has altered the pricing landscape. While e-commerce has rapidly grown, online pricing is falling absolutely and relative to inflation. Price transparency readily available to all those with an internet connection also makes it tougher for companies to extract higher prices on both consumer and business products.

Words of the Wise: While the possibility of a return to inflationary times may be a source of worry in the current environment of very strong economic growth and low unemployment, our global business climate has changed and may bend away from a higher-cost environment. And a vigilant Federal Reserve continues to be hyper-focused on keeping inflation in check and price levels stable through adjustments in monetary policy.

CHAPTER 34

FINANCIAL BIG ROCKS
AND SMALL ROCKS

First, a story from the great Steven Covey:

One day a professor was speaking to a group of business students and, to drive home a point, used an illustration I'm sure those students will never forget.

As this man stood in front of the group of high-powered over-achievers he said, "Okay, time for a quiz." Then he pulled out a one-gallon, wide-mouthed mason jar and set it on a table in front of him. Then he produced about a dozen fist-sized rocks and carefully placed them, one at a time, into the jar.

When the jar was filled to the top and no more rocks would fit inside, he asked, "Is this jar full?"

Everyone in the class said, "Yes."

Then he said, "Really?"

He reached under the table and pulled out a bucket of gravel. Then he dumped some gravel in and shook the jar causing pieces of gravel to work themselves down into the spaces between the big rocks.

Then he smiled and asked the group once more, "Is the jar full?"

By this time, the class was onto him.

"Probably not," one of them answered.

"Good!" he replied.

And he reached under the table and brought out a bucket of sand. He started dumping the sand in and it went into all the spaces left between the rocks and the gravel.

Once more he asked the question, "Is this jar full?"

"No!" the class shouted.

Once again, he said, "Good!"

Then he grabbed a pitcher of water and began to pour it in until the jar was filled to the brim.

Then he looked up at the class and asked, "What is the point of this illustration?"

One eager beaver raised his hand and said, "The point is, no matter how full your schedule is if you try really hard, you can always fit some more things into it!"

"No," the speaker replied, "that's not the point. The truth this illustration teaches us is: If you don't put the big rocks in first, you'll never get them in at all."

This lesson is very important, not only to order your priorities in life, but also to meeting your long-term financial goals. Very simply, focus on the big rocks and you won't have to worry about the small rocks. In terms of saving for the future and meeting your long-term financial goals, what are the big and small rocks?

Big Rocks: Consistently contributing as much as possible to your 401(k) or 403(b) plan. Receiving the full company match for your 401(k) account. Investing these funds in for the long term in stocks, mutual funds, or index funds, and not trading the account on every news event. Paying off credit cards in full every month. Buying a house that you can afford and paying down the some of the principal ahead of time. Contributing to an IRA or 529 education plan if you are able. Driving a sensible car and keeping it for a few years after it is paid off.

Small Rocks: Cutting out your morning Starbucks habit. Clipping coupons. Carrying less house or car insurance than is prudent, to save money. Reusing plastic bags. Making your own Christmas gifts. Driving instead of flying on your yearly vacation. Struggling with the service on your low-cost cell phone plan. Canceling your television service. Hiding under a blanket in order to not turn on the heat. Etc.

Many financial commentators focus only on the small rocks, and state that if you add enough small rocks to the jar, then you will eventually become financially independent. However, by focusing on the big rocks consistently over time, you will be able to not sweat the small rocks, and this focus on the large things will also help you and your family sleep better at night, knowing that your financial future is secure.

Words of the Wise: Focusing on the big rocks will also allow you to have a positive relationship with money. A negative relationship with money can develop from constantly worrying about the small stuff and from consistently denying yourself anything positive resulting from your hard work. You strived to excel in school, got a good education, and are now working hard on your career. You should be able to enjoy your daily Starbucks run, binge-watching Netflix, or whatever your simple pleasure happens to be. If you take care of the big rocks first, then you can eliminate your focus on the small rocks as you will know that you are doing the things that will create a happy and secure tomorrow.

CHAPTER 35

Should I Manage My Own Money?

The next time you drive down the highway, look around at all the other vehicles around you. You will see many Hondas, Toyotas, and Hyundais. You will also see many Mercedes, BMWs, and Porsches. That is because there are a wide variety of consumer tastes, needs and desires in the car-ownership market. Different drivers value different attributes in a car, and every car owner feels that different things are important to their driving experience. Some consumers just need a reliable way to get to and from work, shopping, soccer practice, and family vacations. Their car does not have to be fancy or cost a lot; it just needs to get the job done.

Other car buyers desire and will spend extra money on fancy amenities, body style, audio systems, and extra safety features. They may value the prestige that owning a fancy car will display to the world. And they want to know that in the unlikely event that their car breaks down at the side of the road that they have a number they can call so that white-glove service will come and quickly rescue them. Neither kind of car purchase is wrong. Different people need and value different things. There is room on the road for both types of vehicles and drivers.

Managing your investments and wealth is a similar product-purchase decision. When an investor is young and just beginning her career or in the early years of her investment and long-term wealth growth journey, the focus for that investor is usually on low cost, convenience, access to investment products that allow for a one-product exposure to the complete stock or bond market, and confidence in the stability and good standing of the company offering these products. The focus for a young person should be on starting to invest at as early age as possible, consistently adding new contributions to those investments and allowing those investments to grow over time without trading in and out of investment products based on gut feelings or negative news stories. At this stage of an investor's life, a low-cost, no-frills stock or bond index fund or exchange traded fund (ETF) may be a perfect investment choice for the growth of that client's wealth over many decades to come. The customer does not have ready access to investment advice or a knowledgeable person to talk to, or to seek counsel from prior to making any changes that may negatively impact her wealth down the road. But the products are usually a very low-cost and convenient option, so can be a smart choice for this phase of an investor's life. These Hondas or Toyotas of the investment product world are a valid choice.

However, an investor that is well down the road in her career, one who has come into a considerable amount of money from growth of a private business or inheritance, or that is nearing retirement, may value the additional help and guidance that a wealth management professional can bring to the table. Investors in this group may value a person or team who is dedicated to his or her family and the health and growth of his or her investments. The investor may value the truly personal relationship that can develop between a wealth advisor and a client and may appreciate the guidance and advice that a wealth manager can provide during times in the financial markets and economy that are not so rosy. The client may have the need for estate planning to ensure the continuity of the family's wealth after her passing. She may have a need for the creation of complicated trust accounts and for the administration of those trusts. And she may need the advisor to meet with and educate the next generation of the family to help pass on the wisdom and financial knowledge to her heirs. These are all very important tasks that a wealth manager handles every day and involves expertise that a low-cost index fund company does not offer. An older client with more wealth needs this advice and extra level of service and guidance.

Words of the Wise: Hiring an experienced wealth manager does cost money, but the service can be well worth the cost. We would not dream of extracting our own appendix; we know that we need to pay an experienced surgeon to perform that task. We pay lawyers to draw up contracts, plumbers to fix leaks in our foundation, and auto mechanics to fix our car engines. These trades all involve highly specific skills, learned and perfected over many years of training, and they all involve critical operations that need to be completed to the highest level of competence. Such is the case with hiring a wealth management professional. A professional provides a level of expertise and guidance in many different areas of long-term wealth management, and the resulting peace of mind can be well worth the cost.

CHAPTER 36

CAMPFIRES AND GROUP TEXTS

The next time you think that someone's constant texting with friends will lead to a lack of communication skills, a zombie-like dependence on technology, and the ultimate downfall of society, remember that over history the "group chat" has been an important part of human development and has been going on since humans first stood up on two feet.

In *The Social Conquest of Earth*, evolutionary biologist Edward O. Wilson writes the fascinating story of where humans came from, what shaped us into who we are today, and what social forces and developments led to the advancements in society and civilization that we currently enjoy.

Before there were group texts and party lines, there were campfires. The beginning of human social society tens of thousands of years ago began with our ability to create fire and control it. The first use of fire probably arose from lightning strikes. Many animals would be cooked by these fires which likely led to our human interest in cooking and eating meat.

After learning how to create fire and control it on our own, a small group of formerly nomadic scavengers could stay in one place for a longer time. This led to the development of campfires and campsites, which was likely the first step toward how our civilization evolved into the highly social and interdependent beehive that we live in today. Campfires and campsites became a type of nest that helped introduce the human species to a more social path of development.

The earliest campfires were a significant step towards group bonding within our species. They were common places to share food, tell stories, learn from each other, and begin to form strong bonds and loyalties within the group.

Once humans set up campsites, it became easier for division of labor to flourish. Some individuals would stay at the site to raise young or protect it from potential threats, while other group members would gather food, hunt for prey, and bring it back for the others.

Many animals are born, raised by parents for a short period of time, and then wander off to live their short lives and produce their own offspring. A human social society allowed the next generation to start its own families, stay with its groups. People could continue together across several generations. This social behavior led to a large leap towards a new human society, culture, and civilization.

Campfires and campsites served a valuable purpose for food, community, and defense, but they were also a part of evolution that led to the fulfillment of deeper psychological and spiritual needs as well. There were no books, recording devices or pen and paper. Stories and information that needed to be passed down to younger generations were shared at campfires. That included information and guidance that could one day save the lives of naïve young people. Stories told around campfires may have imparted practical knowledge about the nearby land, vegetation, enemies, and animals. Crucial knowledge was passed down between generations because it was important for survival.

Over the millennia, evolving humans used campfires as a place to tell stories, dance, and sing together as a community. Even today, an actual campfire is still a great place to share personal stories, sing songs and pass the time in fellowship.

Groups of humans with similar backgrounds, family ties and geographical proximity eventually banded together as tribes. Tribes are still an important part of society today and can be seen in the rooting for a sports team, a high school clique, a book club, or a hunting trip.

Wilson notes, "People must have a tribe. It gives them a name in addition to their own and social meaning in a chaotic world. It makes the environment less disorienting and dangerous. People savor the company of like-minded friends, and they yearn to be in one of the best tribes. To be part of a combat marine regiment, perhaps, an elite college, the executive committee of a company, a religious sect, a fraternity, a garden club, any collectivity that can be compared favorably with others."

The social benefits of campfires evolved over time as technology evolved with the introduction of the written word, the printing press, newspapers, radio, television and the internet. Former President Franklin Delano Roosevelt knew the power of gathering people together around their new radio devices to deliver his fireside chats. Although the United States population was spread far and wide and coast to coast in the 1930s, Roosevelt was able to calm and soothe a nation weary from the Great Depression with his thirty such radio broadcasts between 1933 and 1944. Roosevelt spoke with familiarity to millions of Americans, telling them about new government policies, the Great Depression and his New Deal initiatives. While these chats were revolutionary at the time, they were merely a continuation of the timeless ideas of campfire gatherings, harnessed by the new technology of radio.

The common adoption of television into homes in the 1950s introduced a new form of gathering around the campfire to learns new stories, be entertained, and share a common bond. Presidential debates, Super Bowls and the first look at the Beatles were witnessed by a huge number of people and were discussed on a local level afterwards.

The invention of the internet continued the progress of the campfire. Millions of new users began to swap recipes, share pictures, create how-to videos and search for needed information. The primordial flame of disparate old fires was now a global blaze.

This led to the texting groups that we see today. Teens on the same cheerleading team, aging fraternity brothers in far-off locales, and carpool moms all form different group text tribes now, and the information they provide to each other and use can be as important as the tales told and entertainment shared by our distant ancestors around their campfires.

Words of the Wise: While group texting may seem like a novel and scary idea for those older than Generation Z, the exchange of information and entertainment is merely the age-old use of a campfire by a tribe, albeit in a much easier form of communication these days.

CHAPTER 37

WHAT IS A RECESSION?

To understand what a recession is you have to know what *GDP* means and stands for. The Gross Domestic Product (GDP) measures how large a country's economy is by valuing the total sales price of all its economic activity in a year. The sales price of all the trucks sold? That is in there. So is all the cheeseburgers sold in a year and the value of plumbing services, thumbtacks, and heart surgeries. Add up all the things purchased in an economy and you get that country's GDP. The GDP of the United States in 2018 was $20.4 trillion, which is a large number. But in fact, it has grown from only $2.5 trillion forty years ago.

The GDP of the United States, the total value of its business output in a year, is typically in a state of growth. The country's population grows every year due to babies born and immigration inflows. There are more people every year to work for money and buy things. This causes the economy to grow and prosper, but there are periodic episodes where the economy does not in fact grow but shrinks slightly. These periods are called *recessions*. A recession is a period in which the economy declines significantly for at least six months. Usually during recessions there is a drop in five very important economic measures, which are GDP, income, employment, manufacturing, and retail sales.

The minimal period of economic decline to be called a recession is at least two financial quarters of negative economic growth. Typically, a recession lasts from between six and eighteen months. These periods are a normal part of the business cycle. Every normal business cycle has a beginning and an end. But recessions can be times of great economic strife. That's because usually a slowdown in business activity causes worker job losses, a decline in consumer confidence, and a decline in business profits.

Economic expansions over the past forty years have averaged five to seven years, followed by periods of recessions of between two and four quarters. Periods of economic expansions typically last far longer than periods of recessions; although recessions do cause much consumer and business angst due to the negative economic effects on the health of the economy in a downturn.

When a recession is evident, the Federal Reserve will usually reduce the level of interest rates to spur economic activity. Lower rates on home mortgages and auto loans tend to increase demand for these large ticket items and may help the economy recover. The Federal Reserve can also inject money into the economy by purchasing government bonds from the open market. The government buys the bond, and the seller of the bond receives funds that he then invests elsewhere in other assets or loans.

Politicians in Congress can also help spur an economic recovery by lowering tax rates for both consumers and businesses. This gives them more money to spend. Congress can also increase spending on social programs to help workers who have lost their jobs. This type of fiscal stimulus also injects money into the economy and helps folks that are financially hurting due to the recession.

A recession can begin for many reasons, but a recession does not start just because the economy has been expanding for a long period of time. Things that have caused previous recessions include a large increase in energy prices, the Y2K spending binge that pulled forward years of technology spending into two years, and a mania in the housing market that caused demand and prices to rise far too sharply, which resulted in a crash of that housing market.

Recessions in the past were much more common prior to the creation of the Federal Reserve system. There was no government backstop during times of economic strife nor monetary policymaker that controlled the money supply for the government. This frequently led to chaos and financial panics.

The ebbs and flows of our economic cycle usually cause many investors to anticipate and worry about the next economic slowdown. Although it may seem like there is risk and volatility in today's economic cycles, a little historical perspective could make us much more comfortable with the current state of economic affairs. This is especially true when we compare the previous two-hundred years of economic expansion and decline. The economy in the past was far more volatile than it is now

During the period of 1870 to 1910, the United States economy was in a state of recession 50 percent of the time, and the average length of economic expansions was a short twenty-five months. The depths of the resulting recessions were also deep. An average decline in GDP was 3.7 percent. Boom and bust cycles were common. With no government financial backstop or monetary authority or plan, there was the need for private lenders such as J.P. Morgan himself to step in and loan the government funds to head off full-scale panics.

With the adoption of the Federal Reserve in 1913 and its assumption of control of United States monetary policy, our economy became more stable and less prone to shocks. However, from the period of 1910-1980, the economy was still in a state of recession 26 percent of the time, with short average economic growth periods of just 44 months, and average recession GDP declines of 4.3 percent.

Only in the more recent era of economic policy in the United States, from 1980 to 2018, have we seen recession periods that are much shorter than in the past, at only 8 percent of the time, with longer economic expansions averaging 101 months and lower GDP declines during recessions of 2.1 percent.

With the creation of the Federal Reserve, this powerful government body became the lender of last resort in economic crises, and its influence helped to curtail risks of large-scale financial panics before they began. A major factor for the smoothing of the economic growth cycles over time has been the Federal Reserve's responsibility for a dual mandate of price stability and full employment. The transparent economic policies and the focus on a stable inflation rate over the past forty years has allowed economic expansions to last longer and the succeeding recession periods to be much less severe.

In addition to the influence of the Federal Reserve, a shift in what our economy produces has also smoothed economic cycles for the better. During the 1800s, our economy was much more focused on the production and sale of hard goods. Boom and busts in the railroad, agriculture, and industrial segments were common. Our economy has now moved away from a goods economy to a services economy. Services are by nature less volatile and do not depend on raw materials pricing and availability, transportation of products, or inventory management. This shift from goods to services has greatly moderated our economic volatility.

While we may fear the ups and downs in our economy with the resulting harmful effects on GDP growth and unemployment, our economy and its growth and decline cycles are far healthier and more stable than any time in the last two-hundred years.

With the adoption of the Federal Reserve in 1913 and its control of monetary policy, our economy became more stable and less prone to shocks. However, from the period of 1910-1980, the economy was still in a state of recession 26 percent of the time with short average economic growth periods of just forty-four months, and average recession GDP declines of 4.3 percent.

Only in the more recent era of economic policy from 1980 to 2018, have we seen recession periods that are much shorter than in the past, at only 8 percent of the time with longer economic expansions averaging 101 months and lower GDP declines during recessions of 2.1 percent.

Words of the Wise: While recessionary periods are typically short in duration, they can be quite painful for those who lose their jobs, homes, or savings. The economy has always rebounded after a recession, however, and has recovered and gone on to new highs.

CHAPTER 38

CASINOS NEVER CLOSE

When the odds of a game are in your favor, how often should you play? You should play as many times as possible until the advantage goes away.

In Las Vegas, visitors frequently play blackjack as it is the casino game with the best odds of winning for the gambler. In blackjack, the house only has a small 0.5 percent advantage on every hand. However, the house usually wins at blackjack over the long run because it plays every hand, even while only having a 50.5 percent win-rate on each hand. The house never closes, turns away a player, or stops playing after a hot streak, thinking that its luck is about to change. The house knows that if it plays a game with the odds slightly in its favor long enough, the gambler will eventually lose his money to the house. The advantage that the house gains by offering gamblers free drinks is another story.

The casino always has a small advantage, so the casino will always engage all gamblers who wish to play, knowing that the more hands that a guest plays then there will be a higher likelihood that the house will win over time. A tiny advantage on an individual hand creates uncertainty for the house, but with over ten thousand hands there is a near certainty of a house win. Huge casino fortunes have been made on that small 0.5 percent advantage.

Similarly, the stock market's odds are stacked in the investor's favor even more sharply than a casino's house odds. Over the last hundred years of stock market trading days, 53 percent of those days saw the market close with a gain, and 47 percent of those days closed with a loss. With a real return on stocks of 7.8 percent a year over those hundred years, the gains came from holding stocks on all days, and picking up the small amount of gain that a 53 percent to 47 percent odds advantage that the investor enjoys over time.

That 53 percent to 47 percent historical advantage may seem to be small, but it is quite large and far larger than casino house odds on most casino games. According to the principles of game theory if the odds are in your favor, then you should play every hand and be invested on every day possible. The only mistake an investor can make is to choose by gut feel which hands to play and which hands to sit out.

Words of the Wise: With the odds clearly in the investor's favor, the risks of being out of the market are high, compared to the risks of being in it. Betting against the stock market by investing in cash or shorting an index fund is a very bad bet indeed.

CHAPTER 39

READ. A LOT.

Smart people read a lot. Successful people read a lot. The average C.E.O. reads fifty books a year. The average person reads one or two. Warren Buffet has said that he spends 80 percent of his workday reading. Bill Gates says he reads fifty new books every year and publishes a reading list of what he thinks are the best ones so that others may benefit as well, at *www.gatesnotes.com*.

While YouTube and Snapchat may be entertaining, if you want to really succeed in life then you need to read. A lot. Read about the world, business, and different cultures. Read about different careers, hobbies, and about the brilliant people who have come before us that accomplished amazing things. Read about whatever subject you are most interested in.

Read fiction or nonfiction. I prefer nonfiction because to me the world is a fascinating enough place with an endless supply of crazy characters and unbelievable events that I don't need an author to create imaginary places and stories for me. But if fiction is your thing, then go for it.

And whatever your politics or ideological leanings, be sure to read plenty of opinions from both sides of the aisle. Read everything from the *New York Times* editorials to the opinions of Fox News commentators. Read an article even when you are sure that you will disagree with the author or his premise. Your mind may expand for a minute while you contemplate the new information, but I promise it will come back into shape in time. Read to find out what your side thinks. Read to find out what other people think. Read stories in the middle. Keep an open mind at all times. Only by hearing a wide variety of views can you create an informed opinion of your own.

You will never finish a book, article, or editorial any dumber or less informed than you were when you began it. You will continually learn and have more to offer and discuss every day when you read and learn about new topics and subjects. Your life and world will tend to expand or contract based on how much you read, explore and learn every day.

Words of the Wise: Whether seven or eighty-seven, always be a student. Always be humble enough to admit that you don't know everything. And always be thirsty for new knowledge.

CHAPTER 40

GEOGRAPHY AND GLOBAL DOMINANCE

The rise of the American economy over the past three-hundred years and the global dominance of the United States as a superpower today was no accident and it is largely based on and furthered by the amazing geographic characteristics of the United States. We may think that our country is similar to other countries in both size and geographical benefits, but the United States is a very special place. There are five major geographical advantages that it enjoys.

First, major deep-water ports that are navigable year-round are very rare. The country has many severe indentations of coastline that grant these regions a wealth of sheltered bays and natural deep-water ports up and down both coasts of the Pacific and Atlantic Ocean. Russia, for example, is also a huge country with vast ocean fronts, but Russia has very few deep-water ports, due to the remoteness of the population centers and the frigid year-round weather.

Second, the inland water network in the United States is unique and formidable. The Mississippi River Basin and Intracoastal Waterway have more navigable internal waterways than the rest of the world combined. The tributaries to the Mississippi River begin at low elevations, which make large tracts of these rivers easily navigable. Shipping food and goods by water is far cheaper than shipping them by land. This makes countries with robust water transport options extremely profitable when compared to countries that are limited to land-only transport options. This factor is the reason why the major economic powers of the past five-hundred years have been Japan, Germany, France, the United Kingdom, and the United States. All these countries have easy access to large oceans.

Third, on either side of the 1,500-mile-long Mississippi River is the largest contiguous piece of farmland in the world, the United States Midwest. Typically, an agricultural area this large would be underutilized as the cost of shipping the output to the end market would be prohibitively high. However, in the Greater Mississippi Basin, the large bulk of the prime farmland lies within 150 miles of a stretch of navigable river, making transport of goods both cheap and efficient.

The access to large rivers allows farmers to cheaply ship their products to markets in both their own country and all over the world. Rivers are much more valuable than coastlines as a transportation system. They can serve twice the amount of land because there are two banks instead of one. Rivers are not affected by tides, coastal storms, or flooding. That makes them much more reliable as year-round transportation hubs.

Fourth, two vast oceans have insulated the United States from Asian and European powers, while vast deserts and mountains separate us from Mexico in the south. On our northern border, vast lakes and forests separate our interests from Canada.

And finally, our climate reaches from arctic in Alaska to tropical in Florida. It is ideal in all the right places. The large swath of farmland in the Midwest is well-watered. The Rocky Mountains trap the warm air rising from the Gulf of Mexico east of the mountains. There it mixes with cold Canadian air causing ample rain for the Midwest. The Sierra Nevada mountains in California cause similar amounts of rain to focus on the Central Valley, a major source of farmland. And the Appalachian Mountain Range focuses its rainfall to keep the east coast of the country a well-watered and habitable region.

Words of the Wise: The rise of the United States to its position as a world power was no accident. The United States has food surpluses, capital, a massive maritime transportation network, and physical insulation much larger than every other country in the world.

CHAPTER 41

WHAT IS A PENSION?

A pension is a type of retirement plan that provides monthly income after the retirement of an employee. Not all employers offer pensions. Government organizations usually offer a pension, and some large companies offer them, but pension plans are much less common than in the past. That's because of the financial risk to the organization that sponsors the plan

A pension is a type of *defined benefit* plan. A worker accepts a job and the employer contributes money every year to the plan on behalf of the employee while she is working. The amount of money that the employee receives upon retirement is defined by a formula. That's regardless of how the economy, company, or government agency prospers over the employee's tenure at the organization. The employer sponsoring the pension plan contributes funds to the pension plan during that employee's tenure. The money will be paid to the worker, usually as a monthly check in retirement after she reaches a specific retirement age.

For example, a pension plan might offer a monthly retirement benefit that replaces 50 percent of an employee's compensation if she retires at age fifty-five and has at least ten years of service. With that same pension, if the employee works longer and retires at age sixty-five and has thirty years of service, then the pension might provide a retirement benefit that replaces 85 percent of compensation. More years employed with the organization usually means more money after retirement.

A *defined contribution* retirement plan is different in that the amount of contributions over time are defined, but the benefit payout to the worker upon retirement is not defined or known. An example of a defined contribution plan is a 401(k) where both the worker and his employer contribute to the plan over time. However, the total value of the fund at an employee's retirement can vary greatly depending on the investments chosen, the timing of those investments, the performance of the financial markets, and the investor's own behavior while investing those assets over time.

Defined benefit pension plans are still utilized in some areas of the economy, such as for government workers like teachers, first responders, politicians, and the military. However, pension plans are much less used than they were seventy-five years ago. The financial risk of a pension plan is squarely on the employer as the company is responsible for making enough contributions to pay the retired worker in retirement. The pension sponsor also assumes the risk for the growth of the fund's money that is invested in the financial markets for future growth. If the fund's investment performance falls short of an assumed rate of growth, then the company must contribute additional money to the plan to shore up its funding. This can be a very expensive expense over time and adds great level of uncertainty to the company's financial picture.

401(k) plans were instituted into law in 1979, and since then most companies now employ 401(k) plans instead of pension plans. The company still adds funds to the plan, but the ensuing financial market risk and retirement income risk is borne by the employee.

The 2017 statistics show that pension coverage is much higher in the public sector (78 percent) and among unionized workers (67 percent) than in the private sector. In contrast, only 13 percent of non-union private-sector workers are covered by pension plans. The drop in private-sector coverage reflects both a decline in unionization and a decline in coverage among both groups of workers.

Words of the Wise: Today only 23 percent of all full-time workers in the United States are participants in a pension plan, while more than 40 percent of workers contribute to a 401(k) plan. These numbers will continue their rise and fall over time as more workers join 401(k) plans, and less companies continue to offer pension plans. The number of United States pension plans peaked in 1985 and has been slowly declining ever since. The responsibility and burden of retirement planning will fall more and more on the individual over time.

CHAPTER 42

WATERGATE. WHY IT IS MORE THAN JUST AN OFFICE BUILDING

Although the Watergate scandal took place more than forty-five years ago, the shadow it cast over American politics, the legal profession, the role of the press and the powers of the White House is still visible and felt today.

Derivations of the word Watergate have also since that time become synonymous with political and non-political scandals in the United States. Since the days of the Watergate scandal other scandals have frequently been fused with the suffix "-gate" as a shorthand to name that scandal. Affairs such as Contra-gate, Monica-gate, Deflate-gate, Whitewater-gate and Spy-gate all earned their shorthand names as an echo from the times of Watergate.

In the Watergate affair, a simple burglary of a political office led to a massive White House cover-up effort, which eventually reached to the highest level of the executive branch, the Oval Office of President Richard Nixon.

Nixon, a Republican, was first elected president in November of 1968. Nixon had run for president in 1960 and had lost that election in a close race to John F. Kennedy. Although the United States was still slogging through a long and bitter war in Vietnam, Nixon's first term left him with a high rate of popularity. Nixon however was a very paranoid politician, and he still held resentments and bruises from perceived and actual political wounds from earlier elections. He saw enemies in shadows. This led to his eventual downfall. Nixon wanted to ensure that he won his re-election bid in November 1972, and he wanted to leave nothing to chance. Utilizing illicit stashes of cash, spying on political rivals, and dirty tricks against his many perceived enemies were all seen as necessary and proper tactics for him to remain in power.

The Watergate scandal began on June 17, 1972 when five men were arrested while breaking into the offices of the Democratic National Committee at the Watergate office complex in Washington D.C. The FBI investigated the break-in and discovered a connection between the cash found on one of the burglars and the Committee for the Re-Election of the President, Nixon's official election campaign fund.

The election of 1972 was decided before the Watergate scandal drew national scrutiny, and before the origins could be traced to the Oval Office. Nixon ran for re-election that year emphasizing the strong economy and his success in foreign affairs. Nixon won the 1972 election in a landslide, taking 60.7 percent of the popular vote and winning forty-nine states.

After the successful re-election, however, the Watergate scandal began to unravel because of deep scrutiny by Congress and the Senate Watergate Committee, which was charged with investigating the affair and scandal. The investigation uncovered a large array of clandestine and illegal activities authorized by members of the Nixon administration, including the bugging and wiretapping of the offices of political opponents to gain insight into tactics and procedures of people of who Nixon feared or was suspicious of.

The *Washington Post* led the investigative reporting on the Watergate scandal, and two young reporters Carl Bernstein and Bob Woodward reported consistently on the affair during its duration. These reporters routinely met with a secret contact in the administration, Mark Felt, who was the deputy director of the FBI during these years. Felt was known only by the code name "Deep Throat" until his identity was confirmed after his death in 2005.

On February 7, 1973, the United States Senate voted 77-0 to approve the formation of a select senate committee to investigate the Watergate affair. From May through September of 1973, the nation was transfixed by the continually televised senate hearings. An estimated 85 percent of Americans with television sets tuned into at least one portion of the hearings.

By July of 1973, evidence had mounted against the president's own staff that his administration was heavily involved in the cover-up of the burglary and its wide-reaching aftermath. Eventually many members of Nixon's own

White House staff were charged with crimes and subsequently flipped and told investigators of their roles in the cover-up.

During these hearings, it was revealed that President Nixon recorded all his meetings, and the Senate immediately demanded that Nixon release all of these tapes so the committee could hear what the president knew about the Watergate affair. Nixon flatly refused to release the tapes, which set in motion a long court battle pitting the White House against Congress. The fight over the tapes went to the Supreme Court on July 24, 1974, and the court ruled unanimously that Nixon must release the tapes. On July 30, Nixon complied and released the tapes to the public.

The tapes revealed many conversations that confirmed that Nixon knew about the Watergate break-in and the subsequent high-level cover-up from the very beginning. With the details of Nixon's deep involvement in many crimes related to Watergate laid bare for Congress and the American people, Nixon had no choice. Facing certain impeachment and removal from office by both committees in the House of Representatives and Senate, Nixon resigned on August 8, 1974.

Vice President Ford was sworn in as president that same day. Ford gave a full presidential pardon to Nixon a month later, on September 8, saying that the nation was tired after the scandal of the prior two years, and his pardon allowed the nation to heal and move on from the sordid affair. Ford felt that a pardon was in the best interest of the United States.

Although Nixon avoided prosecution from any crimes related to Watergate, sixty-nine government officials were charged with Watergate-related crimes, with forty-eight being found guilty.

Words of the Wise: American culture was changed due to the sordid Watergate scandal, and the tumult in America over these two years forever changed how the public viewed and trusted the role of politicians in Washington, D.C. Attitudes also changed regarding the limits of presidential power and its obligations to transparency versus executive privilege. The role of the American press was also rewritten from being a largely cozy relationship between administrations and those in the press who covered them. Press members took on the roles of detectives and investigative watchdogs in uncovering malfeasance and in speaking truth to power.

CHAPTER 43

WATERSKIING AND WEALTH MANAGEMENT

If you have ever experienced the thrill of waterskiing behind a fast boat, then you may have learned the cardinal rule of the sport, which is keep your head up. If you look down, you will see waves, bumps, the turbulence of the boat's wake, and impending doom all around you. Keep your eyes down long enough and you will wipe out as the volatility and tumult of all that is going on around your feet will shake your confidence. However, by keeping your head up, and your eyes focused on the horizon, you may have a much more pleasant experience and stay on your skis much longer. The horizon is a much more stable view, and you can ignore the danger and glide through all the chaos that is going on around your skis.

Waterskiing is very similar to long-term wealth management. If you have a comprehensive wealth-management plan, a steady and trusted team, and the ability to focus on the long-term horizon, then your wealth journey will be a much smoother ride, with less heartache and wipeouts. However, by looking down, i.e. watching CNBC all day, buying the latest hot stock tip, fretting every market correction, and giving credence to every pundit who says the end of the world is nigh, we take our eyes off the horizon, and hurt our chances at long-term investment success

Market volatility and drawdowns in the form of a 10 percent correction in the S&P 500 are sometimes overdue and are a normal part of a bull market. Over the past hundred years, we have experienced a 10 percent correction about once a year on average. Bull market corrections are quick, sharp, and may cause a lot of short-term angst. They come out of nowhere with little actual news to base them on, and are usually over quickly. They take out the weak hands in the market, and they remind everyone else that risk still exists. However, bull market corrections are healthy, and they remind investors why their wealth plan is diversified in the first place.

As a long-term investor, you are not "looking down," and you may not even notice temporary market corrections or extreme periods of market volatility that we endure every so often. With your eyes fixed on the horizon, you can sleep well knowing that short-term shocks and negative news events are not a threat at all to the success of your long-term wealth-management goals.

Words of the Wise: After the long bull market that we have experienced since the tumult of the 2008-09 financial crisis, investors may consider playing the risky parlor game of trying to sell stocks to cash, and then reinvesting the funds after the hoped for, and inevitable market crash. However, if an investor has a comprehensive wealth plan, a long-term focus, and the courage to stick with the plan through all the ups and downs that come his way, then he does not have to prove how smart he is by trying to time the market. He is already smart.

CHAPTER 44

WHY DOES OUR ECONOMY CONTINUALLY GROW OVER TIME?

From 1802 through 2018, the United States stock market has averaged a 6.8 percent gain annually, net of inflation. The growth in stock prices has been directly linked to the steady growth in the United States economy. Why does our economy continually grow over time with only short periods of economic recession interrupting that growth? There are three powerful reasons.

Population growth: With babies born every year and healthy immigration numbers, the number of consumers and productive members of the economy increases every year.

Technological advances: Americans are an entrepreneurial and intelligent people and we constantly improve on the technology of the previous generation. Technology constantly advances, and we never retreat to older, less-productive means. Once we use an iPhone, we never return to Nokia 5410s. Each generation builds upon the advances of the last as new inventions are created and discoveries are made, which leads to …

Productivity increases: As technology evolves, so does our ability to create more output with less work. American GDP per capita is now about $56,000. In real terms, that's a staggering six times the amount generated per person in 1930. Americans are not intrinsically more intelligent today. They don't work harder than Americans did in 1930. Rather, they work far more efficiently and thereby produce far more goods and services.

And with all the angst about the fear of robots stealing our jobs, we currently see record low rates of unemployment. Our economy constantly evolves and changes. New industries are invented and rise while other less productive industries die off. Amazon rises while Sears falters and fades away. Uber becomes dominant while taxi drivers lose their rides. Expedia. com becomes dominant while travel agents retire. Our economy is dynamic and ever-changing, and capital flows where it is treated best and generates the highest return on investment.

It has been said that there are no pessimists on the *Forbes 400* list of the richest Americans. The United States has the most ambitious, entrepreneurial, hard-working, productive, risk-taking, and optimistic workforce in the world. Millions of new businesses are created every year by optimistic people with good ideas, hoping to build a better mousetrap and a better life.

Words of the Wise: Although the United States has been reported to be "going down the tubes" by every generation over the last 242 years, it has never paid to bet against us. In chart lingo, the history of the United States economy and the stock market has been up and to the right. The future is as well.

CHAPTER 45

WHAT IS THE FEDERAL RESERVE?

Through its powers as a government, our leaders attempt to provide stability and growth for the United States economy. To do this the government uses two types of economic policy, which are *fiscal policy* and *monetary policy*.

Fiscal policy refers to the taxing and spending actions of governments. In the United States, the national fiscal policy is determined by the executive and legislative branches of the government. This means that Congress gets to draw up spending bills and the president must sign the bill for it to become law. When the government takes your income tax payments and spends them on government programs, that is an act of fiscal policy.

Monetary policy is primarily concerned with the management of interest rates and the total supply of money in circulation and is carried out by Federal Reserve.

The Federal Reserve System is the central bank of the United States. It was created by Congress to provide the nation with a safer, more flexible, and more stable, monetary and financial system. The Federal Reserve was created in 1913 and has controlled monetary policy ever since.

Today, the Federal Reserve's responsibilities fall into three general areas:

- Conducting the nation's monetary policy by influencing money and credit conditions in the economy in pursuit of full employment and stable prices.

- Supervising and regulating banks and other important financial institutions to ensure the safety and soundness of the nation's banking and financial system and to protect the credit rights of consumers.

- Maintaining the stability of the financial system and containing large risks to the financial system that may arise in financial markets.

The Federal Open Market Committee (FOMC) is very important also. The FOMC is the monetary policymaking body of the Federal Reserve System. The FOMC is composed of twelve members, and the head of the Federal Reserve serves as the chair of the FOMC. All the reserve bank presidents, including those who are not voting members, attend FOMC meetings, participate in the discussion, and contribute to the assessment of the economy and policy options.

The FOMC schedules eight meetings per year, which is about one every six weeks. The committee may also hold unscheduled meetings as necessary to review economic and financial developments. The FOMC issues a policy statement following each regular meeting that summarizes the committee's economic outlook and the policy decisions arising from that meeting.

By law the Federal Reserve conducts monetary policy to achieve its stated objectives of maximum employment (low unemployment) and stable prices (low inflation). Usually, the FOMC conducts policy by adjusting the level of short-term interest rates in response to changes in the economic outlook. If the economy is growing too quickly, then it could lead to a higher level of inflation. The Federal Reserve can raise interest rates to slow the economy down. If there is an economic shock or a recession, then the Federal Reserve could lower interest rates to spur a return to economic growth.

Words of the Wise: The economic power and responsibilities of the Federal Reserve are broad and important. While the financial levers that the Fed can pull are few, an increase or decrease in interest rates and the total supply of money available in the economy can greatly impact the direction of the economy.

CHAPTER 46

CREDIT CARDS ARE NOT YOUR FRIEND

Credit cards are issued as revolving credit accounts to customers who are both rich and poor. Credit cards are a convenient way to pay for most goods and services in today's society, but abuse of these credit lines can be extremely dangerous to the financial wellbeing of the average consumer. And credit cards are a terrible way to finance a purchase on a long-term basis.

Credit cards are easy to get and convenient to use, but can be hazardous to your financial health. Credit card companies charge extremely high rates of interest on unpaid balances, and the burden of continually accruing interest debt can quickly doom a young person's credit rating, their ability to finance purchases in the future, and a savings plan for future retirement.

Credit card companies charge exorbitant rates of interest, in the range of 18 to 24 percent or higher. They do this both because they can and because they must. The default rate on credit card balances (the rate at which the cardholders refuse to pay their debts and then walk away or declare bankruptcy) is far higher than for other debts, such as auto loans or home mortgage loans. Credit card companies must charge very high rates of interest on all their customers to make up for the financial losses due to their delinquent customers.

The credit card companies allow cardholders to roll over outstanding debt balances by allowing customers to pay a minimal monthly payment, but they are not doing the customer any favors. The credit card companies earn high rates of interest on all outstanding balances, so they would prefer their customers to continually make only minimum payments every month. Due to the high rates of interest that accrues on outstanding balances if a customer makes only the minimum monthly payment each month, then it may take decades to pay off the whole balance.

Many businesses in daily life require a credit card which is used as a deposit, such as when you check into a hotel or rent a car, so you may need to carry one. However, you should only use a credit card as a convenient way to pay for a good or service and only if you can pay off the full balance at the end of each month. If you know you cannot afford to pay the balance in full at the end of a month, then you should not be charging that amount to your credit card.

Words of the Wise: Many intelligent people have been caught up in financing their desired lifestyles by charging far too much to credit cards and have been ruined financially when they realize that they have no ability to pay off their debts. Meanwhile, the interest just continues to accrue. If there is one thing that a young person can do to help ensure their financial success and a sound financial future, it is to not become addicted to the allure of credit cards.

CHAPTER 47

WHAT IS NATO AND WHY DO WE NEED IT?

The Imperial War Museum in London was founded in 1917, and it was intended to record the civil and military war effort and sacrifice of Britain and its empire during the First World War. It then expanded to include the events of World War II. The wars were only twenty years apart and the carnage and destruction that these two world wars wreaked on Europe is a stark reminder of why the idea of a European Union was formed in 1947 and why it is still a great idea today more than seventy years after its founding.

Americans have had the luxury of going to war when we choose to. Europeans for hundreds of years did not have that choice as their neighbors could invade at any time and often did. Peace and harmony are not Europe's natural state and never was prior to the formation of the European Union. Europe is similar in land mass to the United States, but encompasses fifty countries, all having somewhat unique cultures, laws, and political systems. The potential for conflict in this small geographic region has been apparent over recent centuries, and events frequently erupted into bloody and costly regional conflicts.

The idea for the EU (European Union), NATO (North Atlantic Treaty Organization), the International Monetary Fund (IMF) and the Marshall Plan all arose out of the ashes and destruction of World War II and have pursued stability in the region ever since. The European Union was founded on the hope that significant economic interdependence between member countries would make further European wars impossible. With all the talk about NATO recently, some have argued that the idea of NATO is antiquated. Opponents have also wondered whether the United States bearing most of the cost of the common defense of Europe is fair or not. The United States does pay more than its fair share for the defense of NATO countries, but this fact is not a flaw in the system. It was a founding principle of NATO. This is how post-war statesmen designed it. They believed it ensured the absence of a great European power which could lead to conflict. By design, the idea of NATO ensures permanent United States military dominance over Eurasia while uniting Europe under the protection of the United States.

Only America and the massive military and economic power that it could exercise was able to pacify and unify Europe under its direction. NATO's Article V declares that an attack on one member-country is an attack on all members. It was created so that the weakest member would enjoy the same security as the strongest.

Since World War II, United States troops have been deployed in Eurasia to ensure that the continent cannot be dominated by a single power again. The United States has large military assets in Europe, so there is no need for countries there to begin local arms races that could end in war.

The United States does spend 4 percent of its GDP on defense, while most NATO countries spend less than 2 percent. But the alternative, such as when Germany spent 20 percent of GDP on aggressive expansion of its military forces, has been proven to be a much worse outcome for its neighbors and for Unites States security. We would prefer that Europeans spend their money on United States goods and services rather than digging trenches and spilling blood in their fields again.

Words of the Wise: A United States-backed umbrella of security over a historically volatile continent has worked very well for seventy-five years and should not be abandoned as younger generations forget the horrific destruction and conflict of the past.

CHAPTER 48

What is a Share Repurchase?

Publicly traded companies frequently buy their own shares on the open market. A public company initially sells shares on the open market to raise capital, build awareness of the business, and to use as currency to buy other companies or compensate employees. When a company uses excess cash to repurchase its own shares, it can also be called a share buyback, stock buyback, or a share repurchase program. A buyback occurs when the issuing company pays shareholders the market value of the stock per share and re-absorbs that portion of its ownership that was previously owned by public investors.

For many years, the payment of quarterly dividends was the primary way to for public companies to return net profits and excess cash to shareholders. In the past few decades, however, share buybacks have been a more popular way to spend extra cash. Smaller companies may choose to buy back their own shares, but large companies are much more likely to do so because of the cost involved.

Why would a company buy back its own shares? There are three main reasons. It reduces the number of shares outstanding, returns cash to shareholders in a tax-efficient manner, and takes advantage of a perceived undervaluation of the shares in the market.

It is beneficial to the shareholders if the number of shares outstanding is reduced. Let's say you and two equal partners all owned a business that had a market value of $1 million. As there are three equal owners, each share of the business is worth one-third of the total value, or $333,333. If the business had extra cash and one of the shareholders wanted to sell his stake, then the company could use $333,333 of cash to buy the share of the selling shareholder. After the share buyback, there would then be only two shareholders. Each owner's stake would be one half of the ownership, and each remaining share would now be worth $500,000. By buying back the share of the third owner, the remaining shareholders' stakes in the business are then worth considerably more.

A company will repurchase shares of its own stock if it feels that the value of the shares is undervalued in the market. Undervaluation can occur for many reasons. It is often due to investors' inabilities to see past a business' short-term performance, a negative news story, or a generally bearish market sentiment. If a stock is dramatically undervalued, the issuing company can repurchase some of its shares at this reduced price and then re-issue them once the market has corrected, thereby buying the shares at a low price and selling them later at a higher price.

Share buybacks are also a more tax-efficient way to deliver cash to shareholders. A company earns a profit and then pays taxes to the government on those profits. The cash left over after paying taxes can be used to pay dividends, but then the money is taxed again at the individual level. That's because the shareholder that receives the dividend payment must pay income tax on that payment also. While dividend tax rates for individuals are lower than regular, earned-income tax rates, the payment still has the effect of being double-taxed, once at the corporate level and once at the individual level. Share buybacks, however, have the effect of increasing the wealth of the remaining shareholders, but that wealth is not taxed until the shares are sold. Therefore, share buybacks are a more tax efficient way of transferring cash to shareholders.

In addition to tax-efficiency, share buybacks are favored over dividends for corporate flexibility reasons. Dividend payments are appreciated and a useful way to send cash to shareholders, but a dividend payment is usually paid at a set rate each quarter and is permanent. If the economy slows or falls into recession, then the company may be forced to cut its regular dividend payment to preserve cash, and this payout reduction would not be a popular idea with shareholders.

A dividend cut would also signal to the market that the company has significant problems. Cutting the dividend is usually the last thing that a company would do to cut costs and preserve cash. Committing to dividend payouts with steady increases could certainly drive a company's stock higher, but the dividend strategy can be a double-edged sword for a company. In the event of a recession, share buybacks can be decreased more easily than dividends, and they have a far less negative impact on the stock price.

Words of the Wise: Share repurchase programs should continue to be a popular way for public companies to return excess cash to shareholders. Share buybacks also have the added value of taking idle cash on a company's balance sheet and injecting it into the market in support of other financial asset prices. The cash that a company spends to purchase its own shares is then transferred to the seller of the shares, and is then reinvested in other stocks, bonds, or other securities.

CHAPTER 49

NOBODY CARES

He who fears he shall suffer, already suffers what he fears.

—Montaigne

Nobody cares and nothing matters right now.

I mean this of course in the most positive way possible. Your family loves you and your significant other and best friend do too. However, no one else in the world thinks about you or your troubles for more than a minute a day. If you think about it, then this realization is a tremendous relief. You are now free to take chances. You can plunge forward and risk what needs to be risked in order to move ahead. You can be slapped by the embarrassment of failure because you know that everyone who you think is watching you and judging you is actually preoccupied with their own lives, cares, and worries.

You are free to be you. You know that if you try and fail at something at such a young age that no one will notice or remember. Even if your coin turns up tails, you can rebound quickly and in thirty years you will laugh about what tragedy befell you in the past. Or you may not even remember it happening. Nothing matters right now. Failures of a twenty-year-old will become fond memories by the time you are forty, and you will be glad you took that chance. No one talks about what Steve Jobs failed at doing when he was twenty-two. Or Einstein. Or Churchill. Or Shakespeare. We only know of these highly successful people from their successes. Not from their failures.

The mistakes they made along the road of life were forgotten by history. The mistakes ended up as half-written sonnets on the floor. Or deleted software programs. Or highly edited bills in Parliament. Or physics theories crumpled up and thrown in the trash.

Will your novels remain unwritten because you fear someone reading them? What if they are great and everyone *is* interested in reading them? Are you forgoing law school because it will take three years and you will be twenty-five by then? Well, how old will you be in three years if you *don't* go to law school? Are you scared to start a business with your great idea because it may be a failure? Who but you will remember that failure later on down the road?

Words of the Wise: Life is not a dress rehearsal. It is happening now. You need to jump on stage and play your part. Even if you fall off, nobody will care. And you will laugh about it later. Even if you fall flat on your face, at least you are moving forward.

CHAPTER 50

The Dangers of Market Timing

The game of investment is intolerably boring and over-exacting to anyone who is entirely without an instinct for gambling. Whilst he who has it must pay to this propensity the appropriate toll.

—*Economist John Maynard Keynes*

Many investors are unnerved by short-term economic and market volatility, and these fears cause people to make poor short-term decisions that decrease their chances for long-term success.

Let's play a game. Let's say you have a traditional 60 percent equity and 40 percent bond portfolio, and I offered you a deal. I will tell you the exact date that the next recession starts, and you can then make all the portfolio changes that you want to for one week as long as you kept a 60/40 mix. After that week, you can only make additional changes when the National Bureau of Economic Research, the official body of record of such events, declares that the recession is officially over. Would you take that deal?

Spoiler alert: You should not.

The consistent worries of investors seem to center around the market being too high, the economic recovery has gone on too long, and we are overdue for a recession. Investors have cash but want to wait until there is a "significant market correction" to deploy that cash. It may be tempting to try to call a downturn beforehand, reposition a portfolio, and then jump back in when all is clear. Know that even with perfect information it can be a fool's game, and it can damage a long-term wealth management plan trying to thread a needle for short-term gains.

The Great Recession officially began in December, 2007 and the stock market peaked that month. The next year was a terrible year for stocks. The S&P 500 declined 37 percent. However, few investors remember that the price of a ten-year government bond rose 20.1 percent that year as interest rates dropped sharply due to slowing economic growth. The allocation to bonds in a balanced portfolio greatly mitigated the effects of a very weak stock market. In 2009, stocks rose 26 percent and gained another 15 percent in 2010. Bonds were about flat over that two-year period.

The National Bureau of Economic Research finally declared the recession over in September 2010. That was after the S&P 500 had bounced 71 percent off its March 2009 lows. If you had taken my deal, then you could have jumped back into stocks then, but you would have missed a lot of the upside. And unfortunately, most investors who did not stick to a thoughtful wealth management plan during the Great Recession sold at the point of greatest pain, which was in the first quarter of 2009. Many did not get back into the equity market until much later. Many didn't at all.

Our basic human instinct of "fight or flight" is well developed. It's been evolving for tens of millions of years. However, we have only been investing, in the modern sense, for a few hundred years. Most of us are still terrible at making decisions during times of increased market volatility and uncertainty. Our basic instincts are not fully developed for the modern investing world yet, so we tend to do all the wrong things at all the wrong times. Unless, of course, we can develop a long-term plan. When difficult financial market times arrive, it's important to remember why we instituted the plan in the first place. Predicting when the next recession will begin or calling the bottom of a market downturn are not parts of the craft of creating and implementing a long-term investment plan. Diversification, patience, and persistence are invaluable to a long-term investment plan, and they are the keys to a plan's long-term success.

With trillions of dollars in client assets and millions of accounts, Fidelity Investments wanted to find out which of its customer accounts performed best over time, so it commissioned an internal study. What it found was both shocking and humorous. The study isolated a group of accounts that performed the best over time, and this group was composed of investors who forgot that they had accounts for a long period of time. What that meant was that these investors were not market timing; they were not buying high and selling low. They were not investing in the new hot product or the new star manager and were not trading or trying to call recessions and market bottoms. They simply forgot about the account, so they didn't do anything foolish, and the assets grew through good times and bad.

People are constantly looking outside their windows for wolves at the door bringing impending doom. Investors are on the constant lookout for recessions, political upheaval, fiscal policy changes, rising interest rates, higher energy prices, Congressional power changes, and rising consumer debt levels. They are convinced that if we can only predict when bad stuff will happen then we can avoid the short-term pain. However, all these events are short-term noise, and not worth predicting anyway.

Words of the Wise: The only thing that can derail a thoughtful, diversified wealth management plan is the investor himself. The wolf is not outside the house; he is already inside. Only by ignoring short-term market noise and temporary fluctuations can an investor achieve long-term success.

CHAPTER 51

WHAT IS VENTURE CAPITAL?

An entrepreneur comes up with a great idea for a business. She uses a small amount of her own money to develop a product, start a website, identify a target market, and establish a pricing strategy. She tests the market by finding potential customers and makes a few sales. She drives some additional sales to her website by buying a small number of Google ads. Her social media presence grows to a large number of adoring customers. Her proof of concept has been successful, but she knows that she has to ramp-up her business operation's back-office to support the growth that she knows she can achieve. But how would she do that with little if any seed capital of her own?

That is where venture capital comes in. Venture capital is financing that private investors provide to companies and small businesses in their initial start-up stages when they are believed to have long-term growth potential. Seasoned venture capital companies make many small initial investments in many promising small companies to reap a large investment gain in the future if that company proves to be successful.

Venture capital companies typically make cash investments in companies and receive partial ownership of that company. That's called receiving *equity ownership* in a company. Venture capital companies may make a small investment in a new company and receive a small part of the equity ownership, say 10 percent, or it may make a more sizable investment in the company and receive a majority ownership of more than 50 percent of the equity.

Though it can be risky for the investors who invest their money in small, unproven companies, the potential for high returns from successful companies is an attractive payoff. For new companies that have a short operating history, venture capital funding is increasingly becoming a popular, and even essential, source for raising capital. Most small companies lack access to capital markets, bank loans, or other debt instruments for funding, so a venture capital investment may be the best way to finance the growth of a small business. The main downside is that the venture capital investors usually receive an ownership stake in the company, so they have a say in major company decisions and strategy.

A major benefit to working with a venture capital investor comes from the extensive business expertise, industry connections, and strategic advice that a seasoned venture capital firm may give to a small business owner. This expertise can greatly enhance the chances for business success as the company grows.

To be able to receive a venture capital investment, a business owner must submit a business plan to a venture capital firm. If interested in the proposal, the firm or the investor must then perform due diligence on the company, which includes a thorough investigation of the company's business model, products, management, and operating history. The company owner then typically makes a presentation to the venture capital firm and answers any questions or concerns that the venture capital investors have.

Once this due diligence has been completed, the firm or the investor will pledge an investment of capital in exchange for equity in the company. These funds may be provided all at once, but more typically the capital is provided in rounds. The firm or investor then takes an active role in the funded company, advising and monitoring its progress before releasing additional funds.

The typical life of a venture capital investment ends with a liquidity event where the venture capital firm sells its interest in the company. The usual holding period is four to seven years, and then the venture capital firm will sell its stake by initiating a merger, being acquired by a larger company, or selling its stock to the public in an initial public offering (IPO).

Words of the Wise: The role and popularity of venture capital has increased greatly over the past twenty years and will most likely continue to expand.

The cost of operating as a public company has risen sharply with increased regulatory oversight. Many firms would rather seek funding from a private investor rather than a public source such as the IPO process. Venture capital owners can also take more of a long-term focus on the growth and profitability of a business rather than the quarter-to-quarter scrutiny that a public company must continually endure.

CHAPTER 52

WHY COULDN'T WE GO TO CUBA FOR SIXTY YEARS?

Cuba, a Caribbean nation ninety miles off the coast of southern Florida, had been off limits to American travelers and companies for half a century. This ended just a couple years ago when normal relations were reestablished. What happened that caused this unique economic and political stalemate to exist?

When World War II ended in 1945, the world rejoiced after six devastating years of global destruction and death. But a European continent in ashes caused a new land grab. The Soviet Union tried to secure its share of the spoils in land, treasure, and influence in Eastern Europe and Asia. Eastern European countries fell under the geographical and political sphere of the Communist Bloc governments that were controlled by and beholden to the Soviet Union. Communist countries attempted to export their brands of communism to countries around the world, and the western democracies tried to stem the tide of the Soviet Union's increasing influence. A new war had begun. This time it was a war waged without armed conflict. This time it was a Cold War.

Cuba's part of this story began in 1959. During the late 1950s and early 1960s, many Caribbean and African countries saw revolutionary leaders rise up from the poorer parts of nations that had been hit particularly hard by economic emergencies and autocratic governments. Throughout the 1950s the United States had supported Cuban President Fulgencio Batista. Fidel Castro, however, had other plans and lots of support from the poor and disadvantaged of Cuba. Castro and a group of revolutionaries seized power in Havana, Cuba's capital, and overthrew the American-backed government. The United States was forced to recognize the new leader and government. Castro implemented new policies. He seized American-owned properties and businesses, increased taxes on American imports, and increased trade with the Soviet Union. The United States was forced to take action by instituting economic penalties against Cuba.

The United States severed diplomatic ties with Cuba and started to back opposition groups that aimed to overthrow the Castro government. A failed invasion by rebels backed by the CIA fueled mistrust in Cuba, which led to Cuba solidifying stronger ties to the Soviet Union. The Soviets even installed nuclear missiles in Cuba. This was unacceptable to the United States. Nuclear missiles so close to the American mainland put the United States at considerable risk of quick destruction. A thirteen-day standoff resulted in the Cuban Missile Crisis in October 1962. The Soviet Union finally backed down and removed its missiles from Cuba. The world had not come this close to nuclear war before and has not since.

In the decades that followed, economic and diplomatic isolation became the official American policy towards Cuba. Presidents Reagan, Bush, and Clinton all signed new laws and economic sanctions against Cuba, attempting to change the Cuban government into a democratically elected government.

Fidel Castro stepped down from power due to failing health in 2008. Only then did President Obama suggest a softening of ties with Cuba. President Obama planned a meeting with Raul Castro, Fidel's brother who had recently assumed power in Cuba. Raul Castro also signaled an openness to reform relations with the United States. Facing a myriad of economic problems, Castro began liberalizing the Cuban economy in 2009. Even with new reforms, however, the Cuban government still accounted for 70 percent of the nation's economic activity.

President Obama and Castro surprised the world in 2014 when they announced that their governments would restore full diplomatic relations and begin to heal more than fifty years of tensions between the two nations. In 2016, President Obama visited Cuba. It was the first trip to Cuba by a sitting United States president since 1928. American travel and economic restrictions were lifted. After fifty years, the first United States flights to Havana commenced. The United States also built and opened an embassy in Havana.

Words of the Wise: Although a fully democratic government or open system of capitalism in Cuba may still be a way off, much of the animosity and distrust seen for more than fifty years may slowly be ending. The United Nations still sees human rights issues as serious concern in Cuba, but the sands of time may finally bring a representative government to Cuba.

CHAPTER 53

ALL-TIME MARKET HIGHS ARE NOTHING TO FEAR

In the 2014, updated edition of Jeremy Siegel's classic investing tome, *Stocks for The Long Run*, Siegel shows the long-term growth of equity market returns, net of inflation, over the last 212 years. It is quite striking to see that the average annual stock market return over that long period of time, net of inflation, is 6.8 percent, versus 3.5 percent for bonds, 2.8 percent for U.S. Treasury bills, 0.55 percent for gold and -1.4 percent for the dollar. If you had invested a dollar in stocks in 1802, you would have $1.3 million today. If you had kept that dollar in cash, you would have five cents today. Any questions?

The stock market closed at a new all-time high again in 2019. While a new high can cause worry for some investors, an all-time high demonstrates that we have made it through every correction, recession, depression, world war, Watergate scandal, dust bowl, oil embargo and civil war. The market has recovered and has then gone on to a new market high. That's happened 100 percent of the time. That's an amazing record of recovery and success. Sure, there are some wiggles, gullies, and hiccups in the long-term equity market growth chart, such as severe recessions, economic malaise and political scandal, but the stock market has always recovered.

In the stock market's long-term march upward, there will always be difficult economic periods, but they are like the seasons. During the winter, the trees outside are bare and seem dead. They are not dead, however, and we don't dig them up to look at the roots to see what is wrong or cut them down hoping to replant them in warmer weather. We wait. We know 100 percent of the time that winter turns to spring, and nature comes alive again. Similarly, the economy and stock market have seasons. Recessions and corrections are usually short and dark, but then the economy blooms again.

Some have noted that the current ten-year-and-counting bull market that we are currently enjoying is the most unloved bull market in history. Each new high has sparked investor worries about impending doom. Were you to Google "the market just hit an all-time high, is it time to sell?" then you would find hundreds of stories and commentaries addressing this worry. The range of stories are evenly dispersed with dates in every year going back to 2010. It seems as if worried investors have been waiting for this market to crash after every strong advance. They've been worrying since the Great Recession of 2008 ended.

Negative opinions always sound more robust and reasoned than outright optimism does, and there is a cottage industry of pundits and prognosticators that fear each all-time high and want you to fear them as well. However, there is nothing inherently dangerous in new market-high levels. Looking back at all new all-time market highs since 1928, the average return from the new market high over the next six months is a gain of 3.9 percent, vs. 3.6 percent on all other days. Over the next year from all-time highs, the market has gained 7.8 percent versus 7.5 percent on all other days. Therefore, market performance is better than average following all-time highs, not worse. This fact is not mentioned in many of those the-sky-is-falling articles, however.

Words of the Wise: The stock market does not rise in a straight line. But our economy and people have always persevered and prospered on the other side of difficult times. With such a solid record of long-term growth, the only mistake one could make over time is to sell stocks, hoping to jump back in when the smoke clears. If you want to bet against a 100 percent record, be my guest. History suggests you will be wrong.

CHAPTER 54

WHO WAS GRACE GRONER?

I don't know much about geology, but I do know that the growth of long-term wealth is the result of time, compounding, and patience. Just look at the curious case of Grace Groner, who died in 2010 when she was 100 years old. She was orphaned at a young age and was raised by kind neighbors. She later lived in a tiny one-bedroom cottage in Lake Forest, Illinois. She shopped at rummage sales, loved to walk everywhere and never needed a car. She worked most of her life as a secretary. She never married and had no children, yet she had many friends who loved her for the happy person that she was. So, it was surprising to her alma mater, Lake Forest College, to learn that upon her death that she left a gift of $7.2 million to the institution to start a scholarship program for students with big dreams but little money.

Grace did not inherit her wealth, nor did she scrimp and save for decades while denying herself the comforts that she really needed. In 1935, at twenty-five and in the depths of the Great Depression, she secured a job as a secretary at Abbott Pharmaceuticals and worked there for the next forty-three years. In her first year at Abbott, she bought three, yes three, shares of Abbott stock for a total investment of $180. She held onto the stock for the next sixty-five years and reinvested all dividend payments. Her Abbott stock split many times over the next sixty-five years, and together with her dividend reinvestment in shares, she died with over 100,000 shares of Abbott stock. No one knew that the unassuming little old lady had amassed a fortune until after her passing. The head of the school endowment said that he nearly fell off his chair when told of Grace's generous gift to the school and future students.

The story of Grace Groner can teach us many lessons about life and wealth management.

Compounding over time is a powerful tool, and the rate of compounding matters greatly. If Grace had simply invested her $180 in a bank at 3 percent for seventy-five years, she would have died with $1,652, which is surely not enough to endow a long-term college scholarship program. However, her Abbott stock grew at an annualized return of 15.2 percent, and that higher rate of return, compounded over a very long period of time, made all the difference.

A simple plan, executed over a long period of time, usually beats a complicated plan that is adjusted constantly. I would not recommend an investor hold just one stock, but that was Grace's plan, and she diligently stuck with the plan over many decades.

Grace held onto her stock through thirteen recessions and many other corrections, wars, and difficult economic times that might have shaken out many more sophisticated investors. She did not trade her stock, try to time the market, sell it because of a bad earnings report, or get scared out by negative market pundits. She kept her eye on the long term, so time was her friend.

Investing from an early age can make a huge difference in eventual results. If Grace had invested that same $180 in 1945 instead of 1935, she would have died with $1.7 million, instead of $7.2 million. Time is a powerful leveraging tool.

Words of the Wise: The most important lesson is that Grace was happy and probably would have been even without her giant nest egg. Her wealth did not define her. No one even knew she had more than a few dollars. She knew her legacy would be to send many students in financial need to college, far into the future. That legacy gave her more joy as she lived than any mansion, yacht, or diamond necklace ever could. Her legacy will live on forever through the thousands of college graduates that she gave a much-needed leg up.

CHAPTER 55

How Does a Mortgage Work?

The origin of the word mortgage is not pleasant. From Old French it means "dead pledge." Mort means dead and gage means pledge.

A mortgage loan is a secured loan and is the preferred way of financing a home purchase. Mortgage loans are used for financing this large purchase because most people do not have the cash laying around to spend for the purchase of a home, which can cost several hundred thousand dollars. Money is borrowed from a bank or other lending institution, and the funds are paid back over a long period of time with interest. The mortgage loan allows the borrower to buy the house and live there immediately while spreading the large cost of repayment over time.

When initiating a mortgage loan, the lender will usually ask for a payment from the borrower of between 3 percent and 20 percent of the total value of the loan as a down payment. Lenders want the borrower to have some money invested in the house as equity. That means the borrower will have a vested interest in the house, and the borrower can't just walk away from the house without paying off the loan. The borrower is the official owner of the house. The lender remains a lean holder on the house's title. The lender is paid back the remaining balance of the loan if the house is ever sold before the loan is completely paid off.

A mortgage is an *amortizing loan*. In banking and finance, an amortizing loan is a loan where the principal of the loan is paid down over the life of the loan, typically through equal payments over a long period of time. A typical mortgage loan payback period is thirty years. Each monthly payment to the lender will consist of a portion of interest and a portion of principal.

The interest rate on the loan is important. The interest rate on the loan will depend on the current prevailing level of interest rates in the market. It also depends on the unique credit rating of the borrower. A borrower with a high credit rating may receive a lower and more favorable interest rate than a borrower with a lower credit rating. The borrower with a high credit rating is judged to be a better credit risk than someone with bad credit, so she or he pays a lower rate of interest on funds borrowed.

Looking at the math, let's say that a homebuyer takes out a loan to buy a house that costs $250,000. He has a solid credit rating; the lender charges a 5 percent interest rate. The term of the loan is thirty years. The borrower will make monthly mortgage loan payments for thirty years, which is 360 monthly payments. The bank demands a down payment of 10 percent or $25,000. The borrower writes a check for that amount, and the bank lends him the remaining 90 percent of the loan, or $225,000. He has taken out a mortgage loan for $225,000. His monthly payment for the next 360 months will be a constant payment of $1,208.

At the end of the first month, the borrower will pay interest on the loan for use of that $225,000 for one month at 5 percent interest. This amounts to an interest payment of $938 for the first month. The loan also calls for a principal payment to reduce the total amount owed on the loan each month. The principal payment after the first month amounts to $270. This payment reduces the amount owed to the borrower by that amount; after the first month the mortgage loan is reduced to $224,730. If the borrower sold the house after this day, then he would owe the lender that amount. Therefore, the total monthly payment is the total of the $938 interest payment and the $270 principal payment, or $1,208.

At the end of the second month, the borrower makes an interest payment for the use of the now lower outstanding balance of $224,730, or $936. The interest cost this month is lower because the borrower owes a slightly lower amount to the bank. The borrower will still pay the fixed monthly payment of $1,208 to the bank. This month the borrower's principal payment portion of his monthly payment will be slightly higher, amounting to $1,208 minus the interest payment of $936, or $272. The reduction of the interest portion of his monthly payment will continue over time. That's because the principal owed to the bank continues to fall. While the amount that is owed to the bank will slowly decrease over the first years of the loan, the reduction will increase quickly over the last half of the loan period. This is due to the borrower owing much less interest. Less interest means that he will be paying much more towards reducing the principal amount owed to the lender.

A quicker way to reduce total interest costs and shorten the time until the loan is paid off is to make an additional specific payment for principal pay-down. In our example, if the borrower after year five writes a check to the lender for $10,000 for principal pay-down, then it will reduce the amount owed on the loan, thereby reducing the interest payments owed. The borrower would continue to make the monthly payment of $1,208, but since the loan principal is now lower, the interest charged on the principal would be less, so much more of that payment would then be applied to principal pay-down of the loan.

Words to the Wise: While the interest costs paid to a lender can be considerable over a long period of time, most homebuyers would not be able to purchase a home without the flexibility of mortgage financing. A mortgage loan is a responsible use of credit and borrowed capital if the borrower can afford to make a down payment of 20 percent or more and can comfortably afford the monthly payments after the home is purchased. As a general guideline, mortgage lenders typically want no more than 28 percent of your gross monthly income (i.e., before tax) to go toward housing expenses, including your mortgage payment, property taxes, and insurance.

CHAPTER 56

EVERYONE ON TV IS SELLING SOMETHING

The enemy of long-term success in investment management is short-term thinking. Whether it's something good or very bad, rarely does anything that happens today in the financial markets or economy matter. Most moments won't even be remembered a year from now. Often a client or prospect will come to a meeting to discuss long-term wealth management and that client is armed with scary news that he or she saw that morning on CNN or financial business networks.

Investors need to remember that little of what is presented on CNBC or Fox Business is actual news, and most of it will only help to derail their long-term financial success. Remember that everyone on a television screen is selling something. The networks sell commercial spots. The anchors sell their own broadcasting skills, hoping for promotions or more pay. The pundits sell the expertise of their advisory services. Public company managements sell the benefits of buying their stocks. Stock analysts sell their own brokerage company's service. Politicians sell themselves to their constituents. Fund managers sell the virtues of stocks that they already own.

There is nothing wrong with all this; it can only hurt an investor's success if he tunes in to the financial news channels every day looking for objective advice or something new to worry about. Investors who are successful over the long-term drown this noise out. While many fearful investors have a long investment horizon of twenty to thirty years or more, their minds may only focus on what iceberg CNBC says we may hit tomorrow or next week.

While television guests may be intelligent, absolutely nobody knows what will happen tomorrow, next week, or in a year. What we do know for sure is that except for a few short, temporary downturns, corporate profits in the United States have steadily grown for 240 years.

<u>Words of the Wise:</u> Our population will continue to grow. Productivity will continue to increase and be led by advancements in science and technology. Stocks are the best place to invest money for future growth of capital. Since 1802, stocks have produced average annual returns, net of inflation, of 6.8 percent, compared to 3.5 percent for bonds, 2.8 percent for T-bills, 0.55 percent for gold and -1.4 percent for the dollar. Given that stellar long-term record of growth, attempting to time the market based on short-term fears is a fool's errand and can only hurt long-term financial success.

CHAPTER 57

THE INVESTING OPPORTUNITIES OF 10 PERCENT CORRECTIONS

The day you plant the seed is not the day you eat the fruit. Be patient and do not give up.

—Fabienne Fredrickson

When a stock or equity index trades down more than 10 percent from its last high, we say that it is *undergoing a correction*. A decline of 20 percent or more from its last high is called a bear market. Over the past fifty years, the market has seen twenty-six correction periods but only six bear markets. Downside market volatility is unnerving for investors who pay close attention to such short-term movements, and negative performance is always frightening. But the good news is that 10 percent corrections are a long-term investor's best friend.

Our economy and stock market have moved steadily higher over the past hundred years, and that's given investors infrequent opportunities to put new money to work during corrections. Long-term investors must take advantage of these periods of opportunity when stocks are "on sale." Adding money to investments during these temporary downturns has been a great way to enhance the long-term returns on a portfolio. Given that the market was recently at an all-time high again, you could say that adding money to a stock portfolio during a 10 percent correction has never turned out to be wrong. Perhaps that contribution could turn out to be early, but it's never wrong.

Looking at the past fifty years of stock market history, let's say that a new investor began investing in September 1968 and invested $1,000 in the S&P 500 at the end of each month after that. This new investor faithfully made his contributions to his account for the next fifty years, spending only the dividends that the account paid out. The brave new investor would not know it yet, but over the next fifty years the equity market would see twenty-six corrections of 10 percent or more. And he would not know that those periods are ideal opportunities to make additional investments to boost long-term returns.

Our new investor was faithful and smart, but also had a strong stomach and added an additional $1,000 to his investment account at the end of each month after a 10 percent or worse correction occurred in the S&P 500. This decision was difficult each of the twenty-six times that he gritted his teeth and bought. This was especially true when market pundits, financial news outlets, his friends, and his neighbors told him that he was crazy. In each correction, naysayers would continually tell him that the market was due for a great fall and to save his money. But he took advantage of each correction and added more money anyway.

If the investor had not contributed extra money to the account after every market correction, then the investor would still have done very well due to a steadily growing economy and positive stock market returns during that long period. After fifty years of adding $1,000 each month, the investor had contributed $600,000 to his account over that long period, while the account was now worth $7.3 million.

But factoring in the contributions made during market corrections, the account grew to $7.8 million. That is the power of 10 percent corrections. Twenty-six extra contributions of $1,000 each during very scary market shocks grew to an extra $500,000 in the account at retirement. While it may be difficult to buck the trend and go against conventional wisdom, it's a considerable payoff for being brave while others are fearful.

Words of the Wise: While the financial media may focus on financial market volatility and scary downdrafts in the stock market that are hurting portfolio performance, there is great opportunity in going against the grain when there is blood in the streets. Remember, investing is not gambling. You are investing in a United States economy that has grown steadily for 240 years with only brief and temporary interruptions in that growth. It has never been a good bet in the long run to bet against the American economic horse, and it will not pay off in the future either.

CHAPTER 58

WHY DO SOME STOCKS COST MORE THAN OTHERS?

Cost is often not referring to the price of one share of a company's stock. The price that an investor pays in the market for a share of stock is not related to or indicative of the value of the company itself, its earnings prospects, or its worth as an overall business.

If XYZ Tech Company has 1,000 shares outstanding, and each share is trading at $10, the total market value of the company or "market cap" of the company is $10 multiplied by 1,000 or $10,000. If an investor wanted to buy 100 percent of the shares outstanding, then it would cost that investor $10,000. However, the same company could have 2,000 shares outstanding, each trading at $5 per share. The market cap is still the same at $10,000 even with each share trading at a lower price. Likewise, the company could have a hundred shares outstanding or one million; it would not change the value of the overall company. Much like a pizza, you can cut it into any number of slices, and it is still the same size pizza.

When investors discuss how much a company's shares cost, we are discussing the valuation of that company relative to the profit that it generates in a year. If ABC Soda Corp. has a total market cap of $1 billion, and its net profit in the current year is $100 million, then the company trades at ten times its earnings ($1 billion divided by $100 million). This relationship between a company's market value and its earnings is how investors value companies, and how they can compare the valuation of one company to another. This relationship is usually stated as a *p/e ratio* or its price-to-earnings ratio on a per-share basis. Looking at the p/e ratio of ABC Soda Corp, the company has 50 million shares outstanding, and the shares trade at $20 each, hence the market cap of $1 billion. To look at earnings per share, we take the $100 million in net profit divided by the total shares of 50 million to get an earnings per share of $2. Take the cost of one share ($20) divided by the earnings per share of $2 to get the p/e ratio of ten-times earnings.

Generally, the shares of companies in the same industries will trade at similar p/e ratios. Auto companies can trade at eight-times earnings, technology companies may trade at eighteen-times earnings, retail stores may trade at twelve-times earnings.

Why do some companies and industry sectors trade at higher p/e multiples than others? It really depends on the business that the company is in, the profitability of that industry, and its cyclicality. An auto company sells goods in a very cyclical industry. That's because new auto purchases are dependent on the health of the economy and consumer confidence. Consumers choose to buy them as discretionary purchases. However, a toothpaste company sells goods that consumers will purchase in good economic times or bad. Those are necessities and not discretionary purchases. A company in a steady business such as toothpaste may trade at a higher p/e than a cyclical business, like automobile manufacturing.

The profitability of a company also matters to its p/e ratio. Apple Corp. earns a high profit margin on its products, so its shares may trade at eighteen-times earnings. A grocery store earns a small profit margin on the goods that it sells, so its shares may trade at a much lower p/e of twelve times its earnings.

Gross profit is the initial profit a company earns after deducting the costs associated with producing its products. Different companies earn widely different levels of gross profit on the goods they sell, but what is the reason for that? One major reason is that gross-profit margins are generally higher or lower based on how much a company changes the raw materials it buys and uses prior to selling the final product. On one end of the scale, a grocery store buys a gallon of milk from a farm and sets it on its shelf for sale. The store did not change the good or add any value to it, so its profit margin is very low. Many stores can and do sell milk, so the grocery store must keep the sales price low to keep pace with its many competitors.

At the other end of the scale, Intel Corp., the world's largest computer chip manufacturer, literally takes in sand (silicon). By using incredibly advanced technological processes, it changes the sand into advanced high-speed computer processors. Intel earns a very high gross profit margin due to the arduous and expensive process of turning sand into computer chips. Intel owns a high share of the computer chip market. That's because it would be extremely expensive, if not impossible, for a would-be competitor to duplicate its technology, manufacturing processes, or expertise in this field. Not so with selling milk.

Recurring revenue may also increase the profitability, stability, and p/e valuation of a business. Oracle Corp. sells database software through a subscription-based model. Customers pay a fee for use of the software every year, so a large portion of Oracle's sales are recurring customers. On January 1 of any year, Oracle management may already know where 80 percent of its revenue for the year will come from. That's before the year truly begins. On the other hand, Ford Motor Corp. may not have any idea at all who will buy a Ford that year. There is very little recurring revenue in its industry. It all depends on the strength of the economy, how many consumers can afford to buy cars that year, and what kind of incentives Ford offers to lure car buyers to its products. Because of its recurring revenue, Oracle's shares are much more highly valued relative to its earnings per share than Ford Motor Corp. shares are.

Words of the Wise: There are many other different factors that go into the valuation that a company's shares trade at. An investor must always remember that p/e ratios from different industries cannot be directly compared to each other. Just because one company trades at ten-times earnings and another trades at twenty-times earnings does not mean that the cheaper one is necessarily a better buy than the other. Each company and its financial numbers and future prospects must be analyzed on its own.

CHAPTER 59

A PIONEER BLAZES A TRAIL ON WALL STREET

"When a door is hard to open, and if nothing else works, sometimes you just have to rear back and kick it down."

—Muriel Siebert

While currently United States elections are open to all adults, recall that women have only enjoyed the right to vote for ninety-eight years. Although the movement demanding women's suffrage began in 1848, women in the United States had to wait eighty-two years until the Nineteenth Amendment became part of the United States Constitution on August 26, 1920. How far our society has advanced on the issue of gender equality has been a topic of debate ever since.

But how women are treated in brokerage firms has certainly come a long way over the past hundred years. In a July 1902 article in *The New York Times*, the writer noted that New York brokerage offices had recently banned all women from opening accounts, trading in securities, or even entering branch offices to transact business. It was thought at the time that women were not cut out to be investors, and it was beneath their dignity to spend time in brokerage offices.

A prominent stockbroker of that day noted to the *Times*, "In the first place, a broker's office is no place for a woman. The average woman knows little about brokerage. Business instinct is not innate in the woman, and worse than that, she can't learn. Tell her all that you know about stocks and market conditions, and the next day she will ask you the same thing again."

Another similarly charming broker quoted in the article said, "Women investors are sore losers. Of course, there is the occasional woman who knows the market and is as game as any man. But she is mighty scarce. The ordinary woman investor makes an awful fuss when she makes a losing investment."

With such open minds and progressive attitudes ruling Wall Street in that era, it took decades longer for the slow evolution on Wall Street to would bring women to the fore. It took a determined woman to finally break down the door. Muriel Siebert began her career in 1952 working at various brokerage houses on Wall Street.

After seeing the disappointment that the world had weighed upon her mother, Siebert was determined to chart her own course in life. Siebert said that her mother was blessed with a "God-given voice," but she was denied the chance to use it by her family.

"Nice Jewish girls don't go on the stage," her mother was told.

Siebert later noted, "I saw her frustration and decided that I would do whatever I wanted to do. I was a rebel."

In 1969 she founded her own brokerage firm, Muriel Siebert & Co. Two years earlier, she finally had approval for her application for a seat on the New York Stock Exchange. Siebert was turned down by nine of the first ten exchange members she asked to sponsor her application. The exchange also instituted a new rule that she would be required to have a letter from a bank saying they would lend her most of the $450,000 price of the exchange seat. But the banks would not lend her the money until the exchange would agree to admit her. Even in 1967 the rules were stacked to keep Siebert out of the club.

Siebert soldiered on and overcame these obstacles. After a long struggle with the boy's club that ruled the exchange, she was finally elected to membership on December 28, 1967 as the first female member of the stock exchange. She joined 1,365 male members. She remained the only female member for another decade.

She made what was at the time a bold move in 1975. She transformed her firm into a discount brokerage firm on the first day that the New York Stock Exchange members were allowed to negotiate their commissions. Servicing clients with low commission rates was a novel idea at the time, but the practice has since grown over the last forty years into the behemoth that the discount brokerage industry of today. In 1994 Siebert was inducted into the National Women's Hall of Fame. Siebert was also honored on December 28, 2007, which was exactly forty years after her election to the membership of the New York Stock Exchange, and she rang the closing bell in celebration. Siebert died in 2013 at age 84.

Words of the Wise: Siebert was a true trailblazer on Wall Street, and she left a legacy that continues to this day. Just because something has never been done before does not mean it cannot be done. Dare to blaze a trail that others may follow.

CHAPTER 60

WHY MOST BUTTONS DO NOT WORK ANYMORE

A placebo button is a push button that looks like is has functionality but has no functionality at all when pressed. Placebo buttons can be psychologically rewarding to the presser as the action may give the presser the illusion of control in that situation. These buttons are usually seen in locations where the button was once operable in the past, but now the system proceeds automatically.

A common but frustrating example of placebo buttons are the door-close buttons on elevators. After the enactment of the Americans With Disabilities Act in 1990, the door-close buttons were disabled. This legislation required that elevator doors remain open long enough for anyone who uses crutches, a cane, or a wheelchair to board an elevator. Pressing a disabled door-close button will not make the door close any faster. However, the good news is that the door-open buttons still work.

Crosswalk signals at street corners do not work either. Before automobile traffic was so congested on city streets, pedestrians controlled the streetlights with these crosswalk buttons. But the traffic signals long ago became automated to better control and coordinate street traffic, and the cross buttons were disabled. In New York City today, there are only 120 working cross signals out of a total of 3,250 walk buttons. The city calculated that it would cost more than $1 million to have the buttons removed, so they decided to just leave them there.

Open and close buttons were installed in new London Underground subway cars in 1938 and were kept operable for many years. For a while the buttons were useful. This was especially true at open-air stations during the winter months. New trains came with variations on the open-close button idea, but by 1999 it was decided that the buttons did more harm than good. That's because of injuries of passengers, pranks, and anti-social behavior from those commuters having a bad day. The buttons were inactivated and now the only folks that push the buttons are well-meaning tourists.

Words of the Wise: Don't get heated, but your office thermostat does not work either. About 73 percent of office thermostats are dummy thermostats that are not connected to the main heating and air conditioning system. People feel better when they feel like they can control the thermostat in their workspace. That feeling of control cuts down on the number of service calls to the office significantly.

CHAPTER 61

How Does a Stock Exchange Work?

A man asked a supermarket owner, "Who sets your prices?".

"Why of course I do," the owner said, indignantly.

"In that case, why don't you double them?" the other man challenged.

"Don't be silly, then I would have no customers."

"Well, if you want more customers, why not just cut your prices in half?"

"What do you think I am, a philanthropist? If I halved my prices, I would go bankrupt."

"So, who really sets your prices then?" said the man.

In any market, the customer always sets the price. The shopkeeper simply records the price at which his goods trade, and they trade at prices that are set by forces outside his control. The shopkeeper wants to make an acceptable profit on his goods, and the customer wants to buy goods at an acceptable price. The market price is set at where these two desires meet.

To understand how stocks trade, it is helpful to consider how any good or service trades in a market. A producer makes a product but has no idea how to price it in the market. What does he do? He goes through a process of *price discovery*. Basically, price discovery involves finding where supply and demand meet. Let's say a car manufacturer produces a new car that has never been sold before, and he has no idea how to price it. He could start by listing the car at $100. At that price, the car immediately sells.

He says, "Okay, that price was too low. The car sold, but I will lose money selling at that price. I will make the price higher."

He then prices the car at $500,000. After a week of waiting and many people laughing at him, the car has not sold.

That price was too high. Surely, he would make a lot of money at that price, but not if nobody bought a car. Has he learned anything so far? Yes, as he now knows that the correct price of his car is somewhere between $100 and $500,000. This is price discovery. He could then increase the price of his cars to $10,000. If his cars sell quickly at that price, he could raise the price to $200,000. If none sell at that price, he can keep narrowing the range until he finds the correct price somewhere in the middle.

The correct price for the market for his cars is a combination of the price that causes the consumer to purchase a car and a price that makes the seller happy as well, which is one where he can make sell his cars at an acceptable profit. The correct price for any good or service is at the intersection of supply and demand. That intersection is the price at which both the buyer and the seller walk away from the transaction happy.

Price discovery should be considered the central function in any marketplace whether it be a financial exchange or the local farmer's market. The market itself brings potential buyers and sellers together to conduct business transactions. As buyers and sellers meet, a marketplace allows all parties to interact and by doing so a consensus price is established.

The buying and selling of stocks on a stock exchange involves a very pure form of price discovery at its essence. On every day of trading, investors who want to buy a stock and those who want to sell that stock come together to attempt to trade shares to each other. Whether at the 240-year old traditional New York Stock Exchange or on today's all-electronic exchanges, the principals are exactly the same. There is always a middleman. That middleman might be a specialist at the NYSE or a trading inventory on an electronic exchange.

The middleman makes a small commission on each trade that she transacts, so it is in the middleman's best interest to find the exact price that brings in the most buyers and most sellers at the same time. The specialist could price her inventory of Apple shares at $1 million apiece, but she wouldn't sell any. Or she could price her Apple shares at ten cents, but the shares would immediately sell, and she would have no shares left to sell. That's because no one would sell Apple shares to her for ten cents. The best market price for this middleman is the price at which the most buyers and sellers are happy with at the same time.

For Apple stock the best price on a given day may be $220. Everybody seemed to like that price that day; buyers were happy to buy stock at that price and sellers were happy to let their shares go at that price. But let's say that after the close of trading that day, Apple released sales numbers that were much lower than expected. Investors were disappointed in the news, and there were now no investors that wanted to buy Apple stock for $220. Of course, there were many investors who wanted to sell stock at that $220 price, but if there are no buyers at that price, then the price is wrong. That's because the price is no longer at the intersection of supply and demand. The middleman now must discover a new price that makes both buyers and sellers happy.

Her mission is now price discovery again. She may list a buy price for Apple shares of $214, but if there are no buyers there, then she may list $212. If there are no buyers there? She may list $210. Ah! She discovers some buyers at that price. She continues to probe and discovers that the perfect price is $209.50. That's where the most buyers and the most sellers both want to trade. The stock opens for trading in the market the next day at $209.50 and trading continues from there. The price will change during the trading day, but only if the supply and demand balance changes.

Words of the Wise: The essence of any business transaction is to find a price that makes both buyers and sellers happy. This principle applies whether you are trading Apple stock, peach pies, or banana plantations.

CHAPTER 62

THE GOOD OLD DAYS WEREN'T ALL THAT GOOD

"Nothing is more responsible for 'the good old days' than a bad memory."

—*Franklin Pierce Adams*

While media reports constantly barrage us with negative news and views that the world is a terribly dangerous place filled with murder, poverty, despotism and misery, the reality is different. The truth is that the world has never been a safer place for the average citizen. The world's population has never been more educated, and life expectancy has never been higher. We suffer from far less wars. Less of the world's people suffer under autocratic governments than at any time in the history of the world. And the world has never been cleaner, safer, or more peaceful

Harvard professor Steven Pinker is an optimist, but he has the data to back up his optimism. In his book *Enlightenment Now*, Pinker compares today's happiness factors to the good old days and presents some very enlightening conclusions on our own well-being. He notes that while many people approach life with dread and trepidation, our actual world has never been as positive for the life, health, and happiness of the human race.

News reports are typically focused on the bad things that did happen that day rather than things that did not happen. The daily news reports the things that scare us. For instance, there could have been a headline that "137,000 people escaped from extreme poverty today" and that headline could have run every day for the past twenty-five years as 1.2 billion people rose up out of poverty over that period. But you will never read about those statistics.

Pinker notes that compared to thirty years ago homicides (per 100,000 people) have declined from 8.5 to 5.3. Poverty has declined from 12 percent of the United States population to 7 percent today. Pollution has declined from 35 million tons of particulate matter to 21 million tons today. There were twenty-three active wars being fought thirty years ago compared to twelve today. Globally there are sixty autocratic governments while there were eighty-five just thirty years ago. There are 10,325 nuclear warheads in the world today, versus 60,780 thirty years ago.

Pinker notes that despite all its troubles, the world gets better over time. Humanity has made great progress over the last few hundred years and has transformed the world that was a miserable place for most people into a very habitable and just existence for most. For most of human history, the life expectancy for people was about thirty years. Life expectancy today worldwide is more than seventy years and is more than eighty years in developed countries.

Pinker also notes that rates of child mortality have improved immeasurably. About 250 years ago, a third of all children did not live to see their fifth birthdays. Today, that number is down to 6 percent in the poorest nations of the world. The number of people living in extreme poverty around the globe has declined sharply. About 200 years ago, 90 percent of the world's population lived in extreme poverty. That rate stand at less than 10 percent now.

For many centuries, the powerful states of the world were almost at constant war with each other. The last conflict between world powers ended sixty-five years ago. Battle deaths have also plummeted over the last seventy-five years, from twenty-two per 100,000 people in 1946 to 1.2 today. The world has also never been so democratic. The four-to-one ratio of democratic to autocratic world governments has never been that high. Fully two-thirds of the world's population now lives under a democratic government.

Motor vehicle accident deaths are way down, from twenty-four per million miles driven to two. Plane crash deaths are at an all-time low, from five deaths per million passengers flown, down to about zero these days. People are much less likely to be hit by lighting now, from about five deaths a year per million people to much less than one today.

Lastly, Pinker is cheered by the global literacy rate, which has skyrocketed since 1475 when only 15 percent of the world's population could read and write. Currently in developed countries that number is close to 100 percent and is even higher than 90 percent in developing nations. Hours worked per week has also declined significantly. It's gone from an average work week of sixty-three hours in 1870 to less than forty hours a week. And due to the near ubiquity of household appliances, the sixty hours a week that used to be spent doing housework is now down to fifteen hours.

Words of the Wise: While it may seem like that are a lot of bad things happening in the world today, life used to be much harder and harsher than it is now. No, humans are not done growing and improving. But our past successes give us hope that the challenges left today can be overcome by human effort and ingenuity like they have been in the past.

CHAPTER 63

BRICKS IN A WALL

"The best time to plant a tree was twenty years ago. The second-best time is now."

—*Chinese proverb*

During my years as a long-distance runner, there have been many early mornings when the shrill sound of the alarm clock only brought life to many rationalizations.

"Ugh, I really need to sleep right now."

"That rest would help my fitness."

"I will sleep in and run later today."

"Tomorrow feels like a better choice."

"What does it matter if I miss one training run?"

Trust me, at 6 A.M. you can talk yourself out of anything. But to get myself out of bed, I have always come back to the image of a brick wall.

No brick by itself is important. But you need each individual brick in place to have a fully formed and cohesive whole. Likewise, each individual run, day at work, soccer practice, or deep conversation with a spouse is by itself not noticeably important. But as part of a strong, stable, and meaningful whole, each one is vitally important. And a lone missing brick is strikingly apparent and weakens the integrity of the wall over time.

Like long-distance running, the most important part of planning a secure financial future is designing a long-term plan and consistently following it. It must be followed day to day, month to month, and year to year. Be aware that in planning for your financial future, there will be many perceived challenges to your long-term plan. Presidential elections, down years in the market, job changes, college tuition payments, tax liability changes, recessions, and rising healthcare costs might all create stresses and distractions. And that noise will always try to be a catalyst to sway a long-term investor from his long-term financial plan.

However loud the daily economic ups and downs that CNBC chronicles are, we must always remember the most important goal of your financial plan: long-term financial independence. Like a wall that is built brick by brick, the results will not happen in a day or a decade. Reaching your financial goals does not happen quickly; it comes from investing regularly and following your plan on a consistent basis, one dollar at a time, over many years. True financial peace of mind is not attained from flashy new financial products, brilliant short-term stock trading, or a focus on whether the portfolio beat a market benchmark last quarter or last year. The exact investment products that you choose is much less important over time than the fact that you consistently invested according to your plan, and you kept your investing behavior aligned with that long-term financial plan.

In forty years, you will not remember how the market performed last year, how tax laws constantly changed over the years, or what the Federal Reserve worried about in 2018. What you will remember is that you consistently executed your financial plan, brick by brick, and the solace and security that consistent progress over time gave you and your family. You will remember that diligently following your financial plan gave you the time, energy, and security to spend time with loved ones, contribute in valuable ways to your favorite charity or cause, and pursue your passions and hobbies. And you will remember that steering yourself clear of the minute-to-minute gyrations in the financial markets gave you time to focus on the true joys in your life.

Words of the Wise: If you have not started building your financial brick wall yet? That is fine. Start today with a long-term plan and with one brick. No single brick in a wall is noticeable or seems important. Unless it is missing.

CHAPTER 64

What is a P/E Ratio?

A basic and commonly used metric in assessing the potential value of the price of a share of stock is that company's *p/e ratio*. It is calculated by dividing the current price of a share of stock by that company's earnings per share. Nike Corp. reported earnings of $2.49 per share in 2019. If the price of one share of Nike stock is $81.50, then we know that Nike stock trades at a p/e ratio of 32.7 ($81.50/$2.49). American Airlines Group shares trade at a p/e ratio of 7.8 ($26.40/$3.39). Apple Corp. shares trade at a p/e ratio of 17.2 ($203.05/$11.77).

Obviously, the p/e ratio that investors are willing to pay for a company's shares can vary widely between companies. Typically, investors will pay a higher p/e ratio for companies that have shown a past record of strong sales and earnings growth, a high profit margin, and a resistance to the negative effects of an economic downturn. In the example above, investors may feel that even if the economy goes into a slowdown, consumers will still buy Nike shoes and clothes, so its business could hold up better than the average company. Companies typically sell for a lower p/e ratio if they have a past record of slower growth in sales and earnings, have low profit margins, and are much more affected by troubles in the economy. American Airlines Group typically sees a sharp slowdown in air travel and revenue during an economic downturn, so investors may choose to value an airline company at a much lower valuation than the average company.

Why does the p/e multiple that investors are willing to pay for corporate earnings rise and fall with changes in the inflation rate? Suppose I told you that I would sell you a dollar now, payable to you in five years. How much would you pay for the future claim to that dollar right now? To assess that dollar's future value, you will need to ask one very important question: What will the inflation rate be over the next five years?

The amount of buying power that your dollar will lose over the five-year period matters greatly. If there will be a 2 percent inflation rate, then you may pay $0.92 for that dollar now to break even in purchasing power after five years. However, if the inflation rate will be 8 percent, then you would want to pay no more than $0.72 now. And likewise, if the inflation rate will be 15 percent a year, you would not want to pay more than $0.52 now to break even on a purchasing power basis over five years.

This discounting principle applies to future corporate earnings as well. If company X will generate $1 in earnings in five years, a low inflation rate over that time would cause an investor to pay a higher multiple on those future earnings now, and a high inflation rate would justify paying a much lower multiple on those future earnings as the purchasing power of those earnings will be eroded by a high inflation rate over time.

Words of the Wise: In a low inflation environment, such as the one we are in now with inflation over the past ten years running at 2 percent or lower, a 16 to 18 times multiple on S&P 500 earnings is certainly justified. However, between 1978-82 when inflation raged in the double-digits every year, the S&P 500 traded in a seven-to-nine-times earnings multiple range. With such a high inflation rate, the purchasing power of future earnings were so much lower that investors would not pay a high price to receive these lower quality future earnings.

CHAPTER 65

THE SCARY INVESTMENT MONSTER IS YOU

Investors loaded up on technology stocks in 1999 when the tech sector was all the rage. Investors then sold technology stocks three years later, which was after the market tanked and right as stocks were bottoming out. After recovering from the pain, investors bought stocks again in 2005. That was after we were sure the new bull market was leaving. After suffering again through a calamitous decline in 2008, investors could not take the volatility and sold stocks at the bottom in 2009. We need to sleep at night, we thought. After so much pain, we kept our long-term investment money in cash for a few years and missed the next seven years of market gains, which continually made newer and higher highs through 2019. Where will the market go from here? I have no idea. But I know the average investor will make bad decisions with his or her hard-earned money and will make them at exactly the wrong times.

The big scary monster that will ruin your retirement account is not the stock market.

It is YOU.

You know your 401(k), IRA, and other retirement account money is long-term investment capital that is meant for your retirement in twenty, thirty, or forty years from now. So why can't you keep your well-meaning mitts off it, and let it grow on its own? In the twenty-year period of 1993-2013, the S&P 500 averaged a return of about 9 percent a year. But the average investor enjoyed only about a 3 percent annual return over that time. All the stocks we buy when we are optimistic, all the stocks we sell when we are fearful, all the cash we keep because we are sure the market will continue to decline, all these decisions only conspire to reduce our long-term investment returns to far below where they should be. If we could just keep our hands off our own retirement accounts!

Stocks as long-term investments are not overly risky. Looking at trailing twenty-year periods over the last 125 years reveals that there are no such periods where returns on stocks failed to at least keep up with inflation. Could you have lost money if you only invested for two years? Of course, but history has shown that the longer the investment period in the overall stock market is, the less likely you are to lose money or lag the inflation rate.

Humans are terrible at making active investment decisions. Because of our deep-seated behavioral biases, we continue to make well-meaning, but awful decisions. It is our "fight or flight" instincts that do not serve us well in the investment arena. Humans have evolved over millions of years and we are now able to do amazing things. We grow our own food. We heal the sick. We fight off enemies. We order a pizza on our phone. We live to be a hundred. But investing in stocks is a relatively new challenge to our human condition, and we have not developed or evolved the behavioral intelligence to do it well, and we probably won't anytime soon.

Fidelity Investments, one of the largest asset management firms in the world, performed an internal analysis of which of their retirement accounts saw the best returns over time. They were shocked to learn that the best performing accounts shared one trait: these were accounts that their owners forgot they had! Therefore, there were no active decisions made, just steady, uninterrupted compounding of market returns over time. Decisions were not made that most likely would have been fear-based and ill-timed, decisions that would have made long-term performance decrease over time.

But hey, you are not alone. Fortunately, you don't need an advanced degree to grow your savings into a comfortable retirement. You have all the skills you need right now. That is, you do if you can avoid being your own worst enemy. You just need to invest early, invest consistently, and set it and forget it. It's that simple.

Words of the Wise: Don't watch financial television. Don't read stories about "the coming crash" or "the coming boom." Don't sell stocks or mutual funds because you are worried about the election, the national debt, the price of gold, or because you want to buy bitcoins. You don't know what the future will bring. Nobody does. And if you trade your hard-earned retirement money based on fear or optimism, then you will most likely be making a mistake. Just make regular and meaningful contributions to your retirement accounts, invest the funds immediately into high-quality managed investment products, low-cost stock index funds or ETFs, and walk away. Look at your account statements quarterly or annually and then live your life. Your long-term retirement is safe. Unless, of course, you mess it up.

CHAPTER 66

ZIG WHEN OTHERS ZAG

In 2018 a *Wall Street Journal* report noted that a large class of would-be retirees were coming to the realization their timber-based retirement plans were a far a less lucrative investment than they had hoped and planned.

During the early 1900s, many millions of acres of forest in the southeastern United States were cut down and turned into farm and grazing land. However, too much land was used for farming. Farmers suffered through a long period of low harvest prices. At the depths of the farm crisis in 1986, the Reagan administration launched the Conservation Reserve Program. The program promised farmers annual payments of about $30 to $50 for each acre they planted with trees or grasses.

As a result of the government incentives, timberland rose sharply in popularity as an investment idea in the years after. Many investors seized the government's offer. People reasoned that trees would grow, and thus gain value, no matter what the stock market did. Investors both large and small snapped up forestland that large paper companies put up for sale to take advantage of the interest.

By 1994 more than 4.7 million acres of farmland in the South had been converted to pine plantation, much of it in Mississippi, Alabama, and Georgia. But the idea's popularity eventually led to its ruin. The region has more than six million owners of at least ten wooded acres, most of who want to cut their trees and send them to market at the same time.

Many of the family tree farm owners were counting on their forestland as long-term investments that could be replenished and passed to their heirs. But just as these retirees were ready to reap their thirty-year harvest, a glut of timber piled up in the southeastern United States. There were far more ready-to-cut trees than the region's mills could saw or pulp. The huge supply of cut trees crushed timber prices in Mississippi, Alabama, and several other states. It left retirees with a lot of trees, but they had little money to show for their thirty-year investment.

Even the largest investors in the country lost money on their timber investments. The timber glut was also a big loser for some large institutional investors, such as the California Public Employees' Retirement System, which spent more than $2 billion on southern timberland, and harvested trees at depressed prices to pay interest on money borrowed to buy it. The retirement system sold much of its land in 2018, realizing a loss for their overall portfolio.

Words of the Wise: An investment may be a great idea, but if everyone else is doing it also, it may not be prove to be prudent.

CHAPTER 67

WHAT WAS THE COLD WAR?

The term *Cold War* first appeared in a 1945 essay by the English writer George Orwell titled "You and the Atomic Bomb." The Cold War was a state of geopolitical tension that arose globally after World War II ended. On one side was the powers of the Western nations, the United States, its NATO allies, and others. On the other side were the powers of the Eastern Bloc, the Soviet Union, and its satellite states. The Cold War lasted from 1947 until 1989, which was when communism fell in Eastern Europe.

During World War II, the United States and the Soviet Union fought together against Germany and its allies. Germany, near the center or Europe, made war with most of Europe and invaded the Soviet Union in 1941. As Germany lost territory and then the war, the Allied powers including the United States and United Kingdom advanced from the west. The Soviet Union advanced from the east. They met in the middle with the fall of Berlin and the end of the war in Europe.

After the war ended, however, the relationship between the two nations became a tense one. Americans had long been wary of Soviet-style communism and were concerned about Russian leader Joseph Stalin's tyrannical rule of his own country. The Soviets resented the Americans' decades-long refusal to treat the U.S.S.R. as a legitimate power of the international community. After the war ended, these grievances developed into an overwhelming sense of mutual distrust. Postwar Soviet expansionism in Eastern Europe fueled many Americans' fears of a Russian plan to control the world. Meanwhile, the Soviet Union disliked what it perceived as American officials' aggressive rhetoric, arms buildup, and its interventionist approach to international relations. Immediately after the end of fighting in Berlin, the Soviet Union set about to capture its share of the geographical spoils from the war.

By the time World War II ended, most American officials agreed that the best defense against the Soviet threat was a strategy called containment. America's only choice was the "long-term, patient but firm and vigilant containment of Russian expansive tendencies."

President Harry Truman agreed and said, "It must be the policy of the United States to support free peoples who are resisting attempted subjugation by outside pressures." This ideology would shape American foreign policy for the next four decades.

The containment strategy also provided the rationale for an unprecedented arms buildup in the United States. In 1950, a National Security Council report reinforced Truman's recommendation that the country use military force to contain communist expansionism anywhere it was feared to be taking hold. The report called for a four-fold increase in defense spending.

As a result, the stakes of the Cold War were perilously high. The ever-present threat of nuclear annihilation had a great impact on American domestic life. People built bomb shelters in their backyards. They practiced attack drills in schools and other public places. The Cold War was a constant presence in Americans' everyday lives.

Space exploration served as another dramatic arena for Cold War competition. On October 4, 1957, a Soviet rocket launched Sputnik, the world's first satellite to be placed into the Earth's orbit. Sputnik's launch came as a surprise, and not a pleasant one, to most Americans. In the United States, space was seen as the next frontier, and it became very crucial to American pride to not to lose ground to the Soviets in the "Space Race." In 1958, the United States launched its own satellite, Explorer I, and that same year, President Dwight Eisenhower signed a public order creating the National Aeronautics and Space Administration (NASA), a federal agency dedicated to space exploration. The Soviets, however, continued to lead the race, launching the first man into space in April 1961. On July 20, 1969, Neil Armstrong became the first man to set foot on the moon, effectively winning the Space Race for the Americans.

In June 1950, the first military action of the Cold War began when the Soviet-backed North Korean People's Army invaded its pro-Western neighbor, South Korea. Many American officials feared this was the first step in a communist campaign to take over the world and felt that allowing such aggression was not an option. Truman sent the American military into Korea, but the war dragged to a stalemate and ended in 1953.

Other international disputes followed. In the early 1960s, President Kennedy faced a number of troubling situations in his own hemisphere. The Cuban missile crisis in 1962 erupted when the Soviet Union began installing nuclear missile sites in Cuba. Having a nuclear threat so close to the United States would not stand, and Kennedy installed a naval blockade around the island of Cuba. The United States and Soviet Union stood on the brink of war, but after thirteen days the Soviet Union backed down and removed the missiles. But the crisis reinforced the dangers of this new type of cold war.

Tensions relaxed somewhat with President Nixon's recognition of China in 1972. But the Cold War heated up again under President Ronald Reagan. Like many leaders of his generation, Reagan believed that the spread of communism anywhere threatened freedom everywhere. As a result, he worked to provide financial and military aid to anticommunist governments and insurgencies around the world.

But even as Reagan fought communism in Central America, the Soviet Union was disintegrating. In response to severe economic problems and growing political discontent in the Soviet Union, President Mikhail Gorbachev took office in 1985 and instituted new reforms to transform the economy of the Soviet Union, and its influence in Eastern Europe continued to wane.

Every other communist state in the region replaced its government in 1989 with a noncommunist one. The Berlin Wall, the most visible symbol of the decades-long Cold War, was finally torn down in November 1989. This happened just over two years after Reagan had challenged the Soviet president in a speech at Brandenburg Gate in Berlin, "Mr. Gorbachev, tear down this wall!" With a crippling economy, the mutiny of member states, and the decline in popularity of Communist system rule, the Soviet Union itself fell apart in 1991. The Cold War was over.

Words of the Wise: Although there were no actual battles between the two main combatants of the Cold War, the fear and unease that the decades-long conflict created shaped the geopolitical outlook for a number of generations. The effects, alliances, and hostilities of the Cold War remain evident in the global power structure seen today.

CHAPTER 68

WHAT WAS THE DOT-COM BUBBLE?

It was an unseasonably warm 58 degrees in New York City on March 30, 2000. Winter white was just a faint memory on that Thursday, and the thoughts of bustling commuters had turned to spring. All was not balmy in the canyons of Wall Street, however, as the shock heard around the investing world had been announced that morning. Before the New York Stock Exchange opened, value-investing legend Julian Robertson announced that he was calling it quits and would return the $13 billion that he managed to his seven-hundred shareholders. He planned to shut down his fund and walk away. He had been beaten by the rampant technology stock mania.

At his fund's peak in 1998, Robertson managed $22 billion, but he had seen withdrawals of $8 billion over the previous two years, including $1 billion in the first quarter of 2000. His fund had lost 19 percent in 1999, badly trailing the 21-percent gain in the S&P 500. He had lost another 14 percent in the first quarter of 2000. *The New York Times* summed up his predicament the day after his announcement, saying that Robertson "had essentially decided to stop driving the wrong way down the one-way technology stock thoroughfare that Wall Street has become."

Robertson, a giant of the hedge fund and value-investing worlds for more than thirty years, was a casualty of the technology stock euphoria that the prior five years had wrought on traditional investors.

"I'm not going to quit investing. I don't mind people calling me an old-economy investor, but it doesn't go over well with the clients," Robertson noted in his farewell.

While use of the internet is commonplace these days, this was not the case only a few short years ago. Back in 1993 no one had ever heard of the internet. A few techy nerds began to imagine and promote its potential in 1994. By the end of 1995, the internet was a national mania and it was all anyone talked about. It happened that fast.

Main Street discovered the internet in late 1994, and the tech stock mania caught fire in mid-1995 with the initial public offering of Netscape, and the release of Microsoft Windows 95. Over the next five years, the buying and selling of stocks turned from a staid and courtly cottage industry into a full-blown national obsession. Newbie investors boasted about the tech stocks they owned, about which ones they were going to buy, and about how much money they were making. Tech stock investing clubs became more popular than fantasy football leagues for the Average Joe, and cocktail parties became stock tip-swapping gatherings. The new business of online trading brought stock trading to the American kitchen table. Stock valuations rose into the stratosphere. Investors felt like they were geniuses that could never lose.

New companies were created every day with names like Pets.com, Boo.com and Webvan. The number of newly created companies with very short business track records and no earnings surged in 1998-99 with 486 companies being taken public in 1999. Since the bubble burst that number normally averages around 125 each year.

In the past, a company would come public to raise money to fund its business growth, to have a public currency for the company, or to attract a larger base of shareholders. The new shares would also tend to trade around the price of the offering. That is so investment bankers could get a reasonable price the shares for trade in the market. However, the trend in the 1990s was to use an IPO as a branding event. A small tech or internet company would typically do an IPO, but only offer 10 percent of the shares in the offering. The IPO would make a huge splash in the media, the stock would triple in price on the day of the IPO, and the world would now know about that small, unprofitable firm.

Investors fell in love with the future of the internet and the changes it would bring to education, business, and communications, but most investors forgot about the most important thing in business, which are revenue and profits. Most companies were being valued by *eyeballs*, which is the number of people that either knew about that company's website or visited the website. These visits did not generate revenue, but investors assumed that sales and profits would come later if the company could just grow its brand and share of the marketplace. That bright future, however, was not to be.

Although few knew it at the time, the tech stock mania had peaked on March 9, 2000, three weeks before Robertson shut his doors. Companies with slim revenues and no profits soon ran out of operating cash and began to declare bankruptcy. Stocks crashed from sky-high prices to almost nothing in a matter of months. Pets.com was forced to declare bankruptcy only nine months after it went public.

The tech-heavy Nasdaq index declined 39 percent in 2000, 21 percent in 2001, and 31 percent in 2002. It would then take fifteen years until the Nasdaq index would return to its 2000 highs again. Growth and tech stock investors, both professional and individual, lost fortunes when the tech bubble finally popped, and many disillusioned investors have not returned to stock investing since.

Since the dot-com bubble, the technology sector has continued to grow rapidly. Many new companies have formed and prospered, and venture-capital funds for new ideas and products are plentiful. The technology stock giants of today were unknown or much smaller during the 1990s tech-stock mania. Those include Facebook, Google, Netflix, Amazon, and Apple. The one huge difference between these powerful companies and their 1990s technology ancestors is that these companies generate huge amounts of revenue, and reliably earn large profits from their businesses.

Words of the Wise: The seeds of the huge technology companies that dominate the business and consumer landscape today were planted in the 1990s tech bubble. Main Street manias like the dot-com bubble have happened over time and will probably happen again in another industry that can capture the public's attention like the internet and technology stock boom did in the recent past.

CHAPTER 69

Farming for Wealth

A man visited a corn farm one day. Seeing the very tall corn stalks loaded with nearly ripe ears, the visitor asked the farmer, "What is your secret to growing corn?"

The farmer responded, "Oh, I can't grow corn. I just create the perfect environment where corn can grow."

Likewise, the secret to growing long-term wealth and ensuring financial security is to make sure you have created an environment where money can grow, and then patiently waiting for the proper financial growing season.

The long-term study of investor behavior shows that the majority of mistakes that investors make in their investment lives are not due to the particular stocks, bonds, or asset allocations that they choose, but in the behavioral mistakes that they make over time, mistakes that affect both individual and professional investors. We are only human; fear and greed are powerful forces of our human condition.

Investors are typically fearful when they should be greedy, and they are greedy when they should be fearful. Emotions are the enemy of executing a thoughtful, long-term investment plan. Much like a farmer growing corn, an investor should plant his financial seeds and then stand back and let time and patience be his friend. To truly succeed and grow wealth over a long period of time, you will need to keep your investing behavior under control, trusting your long-term plan through both sunshine and stormy weather.

I would recommend reading an interesting book, *Simple Wealth, Inevitable Wealth* by Nick Murray. On the cover of the book there is a picture of a tree. Murray uses the tree as his analogy for a long-term mindset when investing and planning for your financial future:

> You plant a tiny tree in the earth, and a wonderful force of nature causes it to take root, and to grow. You don't have to do much with it: the air and the water and the nutrients it needs are all around the tree, and the tree knows how to use these elements. You don't dig it up every ninety days to check on its progress. Nothing much will have changed in that brief time, and you might harm the tree. You don't uproot the tree and store it in your garage over the winter to protect it from what you regard as bad weather.

> Though its leaves drop, and it stops growing for a season, the tree itself does not die. Give the tree enough room, enough light and enough time. Then leave it pretty much alone. It will give you back air and shade and beauty as it grows – and will go on doing so for your children after you're gone.

Growing trees and growing wealth share the same principles. Save and invest consistently over a long period of time. Plant your financial tree, and then leave it alone to let it breathe, grow and thrive.

Murray also notes, "The importance of individual fund or stock selection is relatively small when compared to the issue of how the investor himself behaves over time."

Words of the Wise: All of the smart portfolio and investing decisions an investor can make can easily be undone if that investor lacks both patience and discipline, attributes that are typically the most important part of growing wealth over time.

CHAPTER 70

THE BEST THING SINCE

While most product creations seem obvious to today's consumers and feel like they have always been in use, a majority of everyday inventions began in the mind and garage of a quirky would-be scientist. Most product ideas were ridiculed when they were first sold to the public. Skeptics decided that the product had no use in society and would not be adopted by the public. The road to everyday use for a new invention is typically a long and frustrating one for the inventor. Fame and fortune only arise after a long struggle.

This was certainly the case with the invention of sliced bread. Bread has been consumed by humans for nearly 3,000 years, and in the early twentieth century, Americans still ate about one-third of their daily calories in the form of bread. Any invention involving bread consumption touched a large portion of the consumer population. As an idea, sliced bread seems straightforward, but the invention of the bread-slicing machine and its adoption by the public saw great hardships, struggle, and marketing hurdles before large-market success was achieved.

Born in Iowa in 1880, Otto Rohwedder moved to Chicago at age twenty and earned a degree in optometry. He later pursued a career in the jewelry business and opened three jewelry stores. With the small profit he regularly earned from the jewelry stores, Otto tinkered with new inventions in his garage workshop.

At that time, all loaves of bread were served whole. Consumers thought that pre-sliced bread would quickly go stale, and it was too difficult to hand-cut bread for mass sale anyway. The only fresh bread for sale at that time was unsliced bread. But Otto heard the common complaints of many women in his town who told him that slicing bread at home was difficult, time-consuming and even dangerous. Hard bread required a very sharp knife.

Otto knew there was a huge need in the marketplace for a mechanical bread slicer. He performed market research to prove the need for the device and to get feedback from women as to how thick the slices should be. A half-inch was the near-universal answer, so Otto got to work on blueprints for his new clever invention.

Otto sold his jewelry businesses in 1916 and began building the first model of his machine in an abandoned warehouse outside of town. For an entire year, he sketched hundreds of blueprints of possible bread-slicing machines, and he began manufacturing his first machines in 1917. But then tragedy struck. His warehouse burned down. It contained all his blueprints and prototypes. Years of hard work and sacrifice were lost.

But Otto did not quit. He secured a job as a securities agent to earn money to support his family and rebuild the capital he would need to reconstruct his plant. By 1927 he had built another bread slicing machine, which was a far better model than his original creation. The new machine not only sliced the bread, but it also tightly wrapped the sliced loaves in wax paper, achieving a long-lasting freshness for the bread, which is what everyone craved.

Otto's machine was built and ready for commercial use, but for many months there were no takers. Bakers did not believe that consumers wanted to buy sliced bread, and thought it was a fad. Bakers also thought the machine was too big, bulky, and expensive for small shops. Otto struggled to convince the world that his brilliant machine was needed.

Otto's only hope was his friend, Frank Bench, who owned a bakery. Otto convinced Bench to give his contraption a try, and the first sliced loaf came out of the machine in Chillicothe, Missouri on July 7, 1928. The product was met with rave reviews from the local newspaper, which described Otto's sliced bread as "the greatest forward step in the baking industry since bread was wrapped." The expression was later updated to the now very commonly used "the greatest thing since sliced bread."

So popular was this new idea of sliced bread that in 1930 Continental Baking Company used Otto's machines to build an entire business around sliced bread, and named it Wonder Bread. Only five years after the introduction of the bread slicing machine, nearly every baker in the country had a slicing machine installed and 80 percent of the bread in the United States was sold sliced.

Otto was the typical "thirty-year overnight success." He later sold the patent rights to his machine to an industrial machinery company and joined the company as an employee. When he retired in 1951, he was the vice president of sales.

Words of the Wise: Although his remarkable invention saw success very quickly, Otto's long road to that success spanned twelve lonely and frustrating years. He could have quit on his dream many times, especially after watching his hard work and dreams go up in smoke. But Otto kept his eye on the prize, and eventually changed the world and many consumers' lives with his grit and perseverance. It is not always the brightest or most lucky folks that see eventual success, but it is the people who do not quit in the face of adversity.

CHAPTER 71

What is an ETF?

A relatively new investment vehicle that has gained considerable popularity over the past twenty years is the Exchange Traded Fund or ETF. ETFs have been available in the United States since 1993 and in Europe since 1999. ETFs offer both tax efficiency as well as lower transaction and management costs. More than $2.2 trillion were invested in ETFs in the United States between when they were introduced in 1993 and 2018. Today, there are more than 1,800 ETF products offered, covering almost every conceivable market sector, niche, and trading strategy. ETFs have become a popular way to invest in stocks and bonds. That's due to their tax efficiency, low cost, and ease of use.

An ETF is a type of fund. It owns assets such as bonds, stocks, gold bars, and divides ownership of itself into shares that are held by shareholders. Much like a stock, an ETF is an investment vehicle that is traded on a stock exchange. Most ETFs are index funds, so they passively copy a specific list of investments, such as owning all the stocks that are part of the S&P 500. Like index mutual funds, ETFs have very low costs and their annual expenses can nowadays be lower than a mutual fund tracking the same index.

ETFs may be attractive as investments because of their low costs, tax efficiency, and stock-like features. ETFs are fairly similar to mutual funds. Like mutual funds, they pool together investors' money to buy a diversified portfolio of stocks or bonds.

The only difference is that instead of buying an ETF directly from a mutual fund company, you buy a share of it on a stock exchange through a brokerage firm as you would purchase a share of stock. ETFs are similar in many ways to traditional mutual funds, except that shares in an ETF can be bought and sold throughout the day like stocks on a stock exchange through a broker-dealer.

Words of the Wise: There can be a tax advantage in buying an ETF rather than a mutual fund in a taxable (non-retirement plan) account. Mutual funds distribute gains at the end of each year, and the mutual fund shareholder is required to report any investment gains from the fund on his taxes the next year. However, an ETF shareholder only realizes gains or losses on ETFs when he or she sells them from his or her own investment account. So, if you held on to your ETF shares forever, you would never pay any taxable gains.

CHAPTER 72

SHOULDER TO SHOULDER

Growing up in the 1960s and 1970s, a common worry of global demographers and citizens alike was that global population would continue to increase to unsustainable levels causing mass starvation, resource depletion, environmental devastation and societal upheaval. We worried that in the future, we would all be packed into the world shoulder to shoulder and fighting for resources, food, and breathing room. Although world population has recently hit 7.6 billion people, the danger of global overpopulation has drastically decreased in recent decades. The overpopulation trend has certainly reversed itself. That's due to a significant, downward trend in the world's total fertility rate over the last half century.

Birth rates are measured by the fertility rate. The fertility rate statistic measures the average number of children a woman gives birth to in her childbearing years. For a country to have a stable birth-to-death ratio, the fertility rate must be at least 2.1. This number accounts for the replacement of the two parents, with a small 0.1 addition for early death from childbirth, disease, accidents and suicide.

The global fertility rate has fallen in half, from almost five births per woman in 1960 to only 2.4 births per woman in 2017. The rapid decline in fertility rates has not been caused by governmental solutions such as population controls or sterilization. The decline has occurred due to market-based forces such as modernization, mass electrification, economic development, higher education, and increased workplace opportunities for women.

Fertility rates in countries around the world can be drastically different due to economic opportunity for women, healthcare availability, and societal norms. Some continents, such as Africa, are growing population sharply. Most European countries have birthrates that are far below their replacement rate, so their native populations, not counting the effects of immigration, are essentially dying. Fertility rates in Europe are very low with Poland at 1.35, Romania at 1.35, Croatia at 1.4, Greece at 1.43, and Germany at 1.45. The German government expects the native population to plunge from 81 million to 67 million by 2060.

The countries with the highest fertility rates in 2016 were all in Africa. Niger's fertility rate is estimated to be 6.62 children per woman. Burundi is at 6.04. Mali is at 5.95. Somalia is at 5.89 and Uganda is at 5.80. It may be no coincidence that third-world countries with poor or no access to pre-and post-natal medical care would have much higher birth rates. Mothers who are not sure how many of her children will live past ten tend to hedge their bets by having many babies.

The world's lowest fertility rates are seen in Asia. Singapore mothers have an average of .83 babies each. Macau is at 0.95. Taiwan is at 1.13. Hong Kong is at 1.19. and South Korea's rate is 1.26. These countries are not growing their native populations at replacement rates, so their populations will decline over time.

The world in 2018 reached a watershed moment in time where nearly half of its countries are in the midst of a baby bust with birth rates below levels needed to maintain population size. The annual Global Burden of Disease Study shows that ninety-one of 195 countries now have fertility rates below the replacement level of 2.1 babies per female.

Of course, these statistics represent both a baby boom for some nations and a baby bust for others. Of the 104 nations still in a baby boom, there are fifty-nine where birth rates are above three children per woman on average. Countries in Africa and the Middle East where women's education and employment opportunities are more limited – a key driver of fertility reductions, account for forty-seven of the fifty-nine countries.

The United States also has a very low fertility rate. Births in the United States in 2017 plunged to record lows not seen in decades, marking a profound cultural shift that could have ramifications for the future economy.

The overall fertility rate in the United States fell to 1.76 births per woman in 2017, down 3 percent from the rate of 1.82 in 2016.

According to a report by the National Centre for Health Statistics, that figure marks the lowest total fertility rate since 1978. Meanwhile, the United States birth rate plunged to a thirty-year low. The 3.85 million United States births in 2017 were the fewest since 1987 as American women under forty continued to delay childbearing. The latest downward trend began with the onset of the global financial crisis in 2007 and 2008, but it has not abated even as United States jobs rebounded and the economy has improved.

The problem for developed economies arises because fewer babies means fewer productive young workers in future years, decreasing the size of the workforce and possibly slashing productivity and tax revenue to pay for critical government needs. Combine the decline in workers with increasing numbers of elderly people entering retirement and funds available for vital resources will become much more scarce.

The good news is that since 2007 the teen birth rate has declined by 55 percent, or nearly 8 percent per year. The bad news is that the only group that saw an increase in births were women between the ages of forty and forty-four.

Over the years, especially in developed countries, women are becoming more educated and have more opportunities for satisfaction in pursuing careers, so they are putting off having children to an older age.

Words of the Wise: Countries that have very low birthrates may see demographic challenges in the future related to a declining workforce and heavy costs to provide care and services to the senior members of society. But the fear of a global population boom that leads to billions of people bumping into each other and warring for resources is largely misplaced.

CHAPTER 73

VOLATILITY IS VERY DIFFERENT THAN RISK

Investing the stock market can be a volatile journey filled with many ups and downs. Even in a normal year, there can be a lot of worry and investor angst about market volatility and what it means for the investment landscape and long-term returns. However, volatility does not equal risk. *Risk* is the likelihood of losses relative to the expected return on an investment. More simply, risk is a measure of the level of uncertainty of achieving the return expected by the investor. Nowhere in that definition does *volatility*, either short or long-term, become a factor. Volatility is a measure of the dispersion of returns for a given security or market index. Volatility is often associated with big swings in either direction, but it is not by itself a negative thing.

It is possible to have high volatility with no increase in risk. For example, a Boeing airliner flies from Dallas to Boston. Due to changing weather patterns, the pilot is forced to move the plane up and down 2,000 feet every ten minutes. While this is not the most efficient way to fly and passengers may be a bit nauseated, the more volatile movement of the plane does not mean the flight is riskier, in imminent peril, or inherently more dangerous than a steady flight. Passengers who sleep through the flight will not even know the difference.

It is also possible to have no volatility but still assume tremendous risk. In skydiving, there is not much inherent risk of not going where you want to go. Either way, you will get there. It just depends on what kind of shape you want to be in when you arrive back on Earth. There is also not much volatility in your journey since you are going in the same direction the entire time. The overwhelming risk comes from whether the parachute opens or not. A skydiver endures tremendous risk with little or no volatility.

While the stock market may see periodic increases in volatility and sharp up or down movements, the market does not become riskier with a higher level of volatility. The risks to companies, stocks, and asset classes are present whether the market is currently worried about them or not. I may be white knuckled on that volatile flight I described earlier, but I am not nervous at all while driving to work. This is true even though my drive to work is much more dangerous than a commercial airline flight. Just because we perceive a risk, does not mean that it exists in ways that will harm us. Likewise, even if we ignore a risk does not mean it does not exist.

The average annualized return on the S&P 500 over the last ninety years is 9.8 percent. Although the market has averaged a 9.8 percent return over that long period, the market very rarely sees performance in the 5-10 percent range in a calendar year. In only six of the past ninety years has the market closed with a return in that range. Although the *average* return seems normal, the range of returns can be substantial. That's just another reason to invest automatically on a regular basis and stay the course no matter what happens during a market year.

Market strategists are asked every December to predict the performance in the S&P 500 during the next calendar year. For the last ten years, the average prediction of the group is 8 percent, with a range each year of 7 percent to 10 percent. Guessing in that range seems like a very safe forecast to make as it matches the long-term return range of the market. However, the 0-10 percent range is the most historically unlikely range for actual performance. In the last ninety years, the S&P has only returned in the 0 percent to 10 percent range fifteen times, or 17 percent of all calendar years. Although betting on this range seems like an intelligent bet, it is not. A much more likely bet would be the 20 percent or more group (27 percent of the time), or the 10-20 percent group (24 percent of the time).

Although stock market performance can vary greatly year by year, it is actually very difficult to pick a month in the past, invest in the market, and then lose money over the next five years. Since D-Day in June 1944, there have been 893 months. If an investor invested money at the end of each of those months and held it for the next five years, then they lost money only 16 percent of the time over the succeeding five-year period. In fact, in only 8 percent of those periods did an investor see a loss for the five years of more than 10 percent.

Words of the Wise: It is very important to keep your focus on the long-term goal of growing wealth over time and to do so without being frightened or scared out of the market by temporary volatility. Investing in stocks has proven to be the best way to grow wealth over time and beat inflation, so learning to focus on the differences between volatility and risk is paramount to your long-term investing success.

CHAPTER 74

THE WORST YEAR TO BE ALIVE

Although the world may seem tumultuous these days with terrorist bombings, mass shootings, increasing economic inequality, and a divisive political climate, our world today is a far more hospitable place than in the past.

If we think back through history to try to identify the worst year to be alive, then we may consider that it would be 1943. That's when World War II engulfed the world and the Holocaust ravaged the Jewish population. Or we may conclude that it was 1918. During that year the Spanish Flu infected 500 million people worldwide, leading to between 50 and 100 million deaths. Or we could say that a very bad year was 1349, which was when the Black Plague was in the middle of killing 50 million people in Europe, or 60 percent of the continent's population.

These are all valid guesses, but *Science* magazine has reviewed the last few millennia and concluded that A.D. 536 was the worst year in history to be alive. Little was known about this period until recently. People called that time period the Dark Ages, and it turns out they did so for good reason. The Dark Ages was a historical periodization traditionally referring to the Middle Ages that asserts that a demographic, cultural, and economic deterioration occurred in Western Europe following the decline of the Roman Empire and lasted until the Renaissance period commenced in the fourteenth century.

A strange fog plunged Europe, the Middle East and parts of Asia into darkness, both day and night, for eighteen months. People at the time had very limited understanding of science and weather, and had no communication. Citizens could only guess as to why the sun was no longer shining. Many concluded that an angered god was punishing humans for their wickedness. Temperatures in the summer of 536 dropped two degrees, which brought on the coldest decade in 2,300 years. Crops failed due to the cold that year, global food supplies plunged, and people around the world starved. Many people were only put out of their misery in A.D. 541 when a bubonic plague struck many populous cities around the globe.

Although historians were aware that the middle of the sixth century was a dark time for both the planet and its citizens, the reasons for the darkness were not clear until recently. Recently, an ultraprecise analysis of ice from a Swiss glacier by a team led by Michael McCormick and glaciologist Paul Mayewski at the Climate Change Institute of The University of Maine determined the source of the global catastrophe.

This scientist recently performed an exhausting analysis of an ice core that revealed the dark secrets of the past. Digging down into the ice inch by inch reveals as much data about climate conditions in the past as cutting down a large tree and inspecting its rings. The scientists can analyze each slice of the glacier, ascertain its year, and take chemical samples of the ice to note the compounds present in each slice. The scientific team concluded that a cataclysmic volcanic eruption in Iceland spewed ash across the Northern Hemisphere in 536. Two other large explosions followed the first in 540 and 547. The massive, global-climate-changing events plunged the planet into economic stagnation that was not relieved until A.D. 640.

When a volcano erupts, it spews sulfur, bismuth, and other noxious substances high into the atmosphere, creating a long-lasting haze that reflects the sun's light back into space. This cools the planet and creates a tragic outcome for those unfortunate souls alive at the time. By matching tree rings with ice samples, scientists at the University of Bern discovered that nearly every unusually cold summer over the past 2,500 years was preceded by a large volcanic explosion incident.

The ice sample from 640 showed a high level of lead ore in its chemical makeup. This was good news. Silver was smelted from lead ore, which indicated that European economies had rebounded from the long dark period, and economic activity had rebounded with the wide demand for silver for both industrial production and for use as silver coins in a thriving economy.

Lead also was missing from the ice samples from 1349-1353, which was when the Black Plague ravaged the population.

<u>Words of the Wise:</u> While we may feel like we are living in a very complicated world filled with disease, terror, and war, just be glad you were not born in 536.

CHAPTER 75

WHAT ARE DIVIDENDS?

When an investor owns shares of a public company, that investor is just one of many owners of that company. A *dividend* is a payment of a portion of the investor's share of the profits generated by that company. If a company earns a profit of $1, then that company has the choice of how much of that $1 to pay out to shareholders. Companies typically do not pay out all their profits as dividends. That's because profits are kept at the company and reinvested into growing the business, so the company can earn a higher profit in the future. The company can use the profits they do not pay to shareholders to build a new manufacturing plant, to buy new equipment, or to buy another company who has a product or technology that will make the acquiring company better and more profitable.

Dividends are quoted and paid on a per share basis. If you own one share of a company and that company's stock price trades at $25, then the dividend payment may be $1 per share per year. Also quoted is the stock's *dividend yield*. The dividend yield is how much dividend is paid per share per year as a percentage. In this case, the dividend yield is the $1 dividend divided by the $25 share price, or $1/$25 or 4 percent. Dividend payments are usually paid on a quarterly basis, to all shareholders who own shares of the stock on a stated date.

There is tremendous information content in dividend yield levels. The S&P 500 yields 1.8 percent today, but within the five-hundred stocks of the index are many different dividend yields and for many different reasons. Utility stocks have an average yield of 3.5 percent, much higher than the index average because these companies generate steady profits that are paid out to shareholders. However, utility companies usually do not generate much revenue or earnings growth, so a high dividend yield is the main reason why an investor would hold the stock of such a low-growth company.

On the other end of the spectrum, a small technology or biotech company may not generate much net profit and invest any profit and cash in the bank back into the business to grow its earnings over time. Investors in these companies are focused on the future growth of the company, and do not require or expect current dividend payments.

Words of the Wise: While dividend payments may provide a nice bit of extra income in addition to the potential for growth in the share price of a stock, equity investors generally do not purchase shares of a stock solely based on the yield of the dividend. Primary attention should be paid to the health of the underlying business, the growth prospects of the company and its ability to weather economic downturns. The payment of a dividend is usually a secondary attribute in assessing the attractiveness of an equity investment in a public company.

CHAPTER 76

AMAZON.BOMB

"I never make predictions, especially about the future"

—Yogi Berra

The future potential and adoption of business and consumer products is notoriously difficult to predict and has been since the advent of commerce. The invention of the light bulb, the telephone, telegraph, automobile, radio, television, and computer were all met with skepticism at their inceptions. The general public just could not foresee any use for these newfangled contraptions. Business history is made, however, by the small number of true visionaries that can both see the future need for their innovative products and imagine how their brainchildren could reach the stage of mass adoption. Jeff Bezos is one of business history's true visionaries, but like many trailblazers of the past, his vision for the viability of his products and services was also met with scathing criticism at the time.

Bezos became the richest man on the planet in 2018. He is arguably the richest man in history. He is now celebrated as a business genius and is seen as a man with visions of the future that scan a horizon far greater than the average business expert. He founded Amazon in 1995 and remains owner of a 20 percent stake. Amazon generated revenue of $234 billion in 2018, which is a 31 percent increase over 2017's revenue. Amazon's tentacles reach from online shopping to book self-publishing. It involves data centers and web hosting, web-enabled content streaming, robotics and even has Amazon Go self-checkout convenience stores. It seems as if Amazon has always been a beloved and respected part of corporate American. It was not always thus.

Jeff Bezos did what many people only dream of doing. He chucked a high-paying, stable job to become his own boss and seek his fortune as an internet pioneer.

In a humorously fascinating article from May 1999, the well-respected financial weekly financial newspaper *Barron's* printed a cover story entitled "Amazon.bomb," positing the impending doom of the fledgling web retailer. Through the lens of the two decades hence, it is easy to second guess the criticism of the company that was laid out in the article. But the degree of lack of vision, the misreading of the market and competition, and the underestimation of Bezos' long-term vision is truly breathtaking. *Barron's* was seemingly implying that Amazon was nary a year from fading into the dustbin of history as the most-hyped business failures ever.

Some of the interesting points the article made included:

Increasingly, Amazon's strategy is looking like the dim-bulb businessman who loses money on every sale but tries to make it up by making more sales.

Once Walmart decides to go after Amazon, there's no contest. Walmart has resources Amazon can't even dream about.

Unfortunately for Bezos, Amazon is now entering a stage in which investors will be less willing to rely on his charisma and more demanding of answers to tough questions like, "When will this company actually turn a profit?" and "How will Amazon triumph over a slew of new competitors who have deep pockets and new technologies?"

AOL has amassed what's considered to be the biggest audience of users on the internet, 16 million subscribers in all. Amazon has only half that many clients, and most view the site as a retailer rather than as a source of information or entertainment. That's why they don't tend to hang out on the Amazon site for hours at a time the way they do at AOL.

Despite all the hoopla surrounding Amazon, Bezos has not really revolutionized the book industry at all. He is a middleman, and he will likely be outflanked by companies that sell their wares directly to consumers. To begin with, publishing houses themselves could sell their books online. And new technologies promise to cut costs even further by allowing consumers to download books via the internet. Books can be printed out on traditional computer printers or put into a new notebook-sized computer device that displays books on its screen a page at a time.

Here's another potential threat to Amazon: What's to stop famous authors from establishing their own websites to sell their books? If Madonna can have her own record label, the theory goes, why can't Stephen King or Danielle Steel have their own book imprint?

Against this backdrop, Amazon is looking more and more like a traditional retailer, complete with an expensive network of warehouses loaded down with inventory. Amazon is buying a lot of costly bricks and mortar, the very stuff that is supposedly bloating costs at traditional retailers.

Those traditional retailers, meanwhile, are moving onto Amazon's turf. Even Borders, the bookstore chain that has been the farthest behind in the race to capture online eyeballs on the internet, just announced a cross-marketing agreement with internet upstart About. com. [Note: Borders and About.com are no longer in business.]

Soon Amazon will be encountering competition on the internet from even the nation's mom-and-pop bookstores. By August, the American Booksellers Association will launch BookSense.com, a program that will let local stores launch individual websites with their own logos, designs and book reviews. [BookSense.com is no longer in business.]

Adding to the cutthroat competition are various websites with search engines that track down whatever book you want at the lowest price. On top of all that, there's the site called Buybooks.com, which has a stated business plan of undercutting Amazon's prices by at least 10 percent. [Buybooks.com is no longer in business.]

Adding to Amazon's woes is its recent purchase of warehouse space. Traditional booksellers like Barnes & Noble and Borders already have warehouses around the country. Taken together, Ingram and Barnes & Noble have enough distribution sites to offer overnight delivery at no extra cost to about 80 percent of the United States The best Amazon can offer right now is delivery in three to seven business days, and that's if it has the book in stock. [Amazon can now deliver every product within hours, if needed.]

Eventually, shareholders and bond buyers will wise up.

Words of the Wise: Dim-bulb businessman? Amazon 1, *Barron's* 0

CHAPTER 77

STAY TO THE RIGHT

About 35 percent of the world's population drives on the left-hand side of the road, which is also known in the United States as the wrong side of the road. The countries that currently still drive on the left side are mainly former British colonies, but global evolution of right-hand side and left–hand side driving is long and much more complicated than it would seem.

During much of history, everyone rode their horses on the left side of the road. Men carried swords, and since most people are right-handed, the sword sat on their left hips, so they could swing the sword with the right hand at any attacker that approached. It would also be very difficult to mount a horse from the right side of the horse with a sword on your left hip. It is much easier for most people to mount a horse from the left side. If most people mount a horse from the left side, then it is much safer to ride on the left side of the road rather than mounting a horse on the traffic side.

However, things changed in the late 1700s. Wagon drivers in France began hauling goods and farm products in large wagons that were pulled by a team of horses. The driver would sit on the horse at the left rear so that he could whip the reins with his right hand. As the driver was sitting on the left, he preferred to drive on the right side of the road in order to make sure his horses and wagons stayed clear of oncoming traffic. The era of right-side driving had begun.

The French Revolution of 1789 was also a significant factor that gave rise to right-side driving in Europe. Prior to the uprising of the people in France, the nobility would typically be driven in coaches on the left side of the road, even while it was the custom for the general citizenry to drive on the right side. When a royal coach approached, anyone coming towards it was forced to move to their left, to let the privileged royalty pass. After the revolution, however, the privileged in society wanted to keep a much lower profile, lest they lose their heads, so they then began following the right side of the road custom also, and the right side of the road driving was enacted by law in France in 1794.

Napoleon's conquests in Europe then spread the use of the right side of the road to many countries such as Belgium, Poland, Germany, Spain, and Italy. The countries that resisted Napoleon's bid for dominance in Europe were areas such as Great Britain, the Austrio-Hungarian Empire, and Portugal. They also kept their edict for left-hand-side driving in place. Left-handed driving was made mandatory in Britain in 1835, and all the countries that were part of the British Empire followed that lead.

Japan was never part of the British Empire, but its residents drive on the left-side to this day. In 1872, Japan's first railway was built with technical and construction help from Britain. Those railways were designed and built to be run on the left side of the road.

In the early days of the British colonization of North America, horses and wagons drove on the customarily British left side of the road. However, after the revolutionary colonies declared independence from Britain in 1776, the new nation was anxious to cast off any customs pressed onto them by their former overlords, so state governments changed their roads to right-hand-side driving. The first law requiring drivers to drive on the right side was passed by Pennsylvania in 1792 and many other states soon followed suit.

As automobile production in the United States rose to global dominance after Henry Ford standardized mass production of the Model T in 1908, many remaining non-British countries were force to move their driving standard to the right side of the road. That's because all early Ford models were built in the United States. That meant that their steering wheels were on the left sides of the cars.

Words of the Wise: While there has been a lot of change over the years regarding which countries drive on which side of the road, in 2018 there are countries that had past connection to Britain that still drive on the left side. And then there's everyone else.

CHAPTER 78

THE GLOBAL DOMINANCE OF THE DOLLAR

The United States dollar is the world's reserve currency, meaning that it is the most widely used and important unit of monetary exchange in the world. We make transactions in United States dollars every day, but we may not realize how unique and special it is to have and use the dominant global currency, and how important it is to our citizens, businesses, and our standing in the global economy. In the movies, criminals demand ransom in dollars. The global drug trade transacts in dollars. The global oil market is based on dollars per barrel.

Because of the role of the United States dollar as the world's reserve currency, Americans can be insulated from the ebbs and flows of global currency values and its effects on global investment and trade markets. While the dollar has reigned supreme for nearly a hundred years in the role of global trade currency, it was not always the case. Until World War One, London was the capital of world finance, and the British Pound Sterling was the world's reserve currency and had been for a very long time.

Only due to the havoc that two world wars took on Great Britain and its place in the world as the credit, trade, and finance master did the United States financial system and the dollar rise to power as the world's reserve currency to displace the influence of the British Pound. Through the two world wars, the United States assumed the powerful role of exporter of agriculture and industrial machinery and became a large creditor to finance the war efforts for our allies. The needs from Europe for financing caused the shift to New York as the capital of word finance as lender, insurer, and capital of the foreign trade acceptance market.

The global trade acceptance market is a little known but very important function in global trade. A grain seller in 1890 New York may have contracted to sell a shipload of wheat to a European buyer. However, the ship may have taken two months to get there, and the cash payment may have taken two additional months to get back to the seller. That large time lag was and is a big hindrance to a functioning business. In stepped a New York bank, who with confidence in the credit of the wheat buyer to send back the payment advanced the full payment to the shipper to avoid him being short both the wheat and the payment for four months. It was this ability to provide the grease in the global trade machine that most led to the rise of America as the world's financial capital and the dollar as the world's most used currency.

The dollar remains far and away the most important currency for billing and settling of international transactions. South Korea and Thailand set the prices of more than 80 percent of their trade in dollars, despite only 20 percent of their exports being sold to American buyers. The dollar is used in 85 percent of all foreign exchange transactions worldwide. And global foreign banks hold more than 60 percent of their foreign currency reserves in dollars. A currency is attractive to the market if the country that backs it is large, wealthy, and consistently grows at a strong rate. The currency is also a strong and a desirable store of wealth if the country standing behind it is strong, secure and a trusted place to do business.

Words to the Wise: The United States remains the largest and most economically dynamic country in the world and has the largest, most robust, and liquid financial markets in the world. While someday financial mismanagement or global crises may cause the decline in the use of the dollar as the main currency for global transactions, that time seems to be a long way off and would take a considerable change in the balance of economic, military, and credit-rating power for another nation's currency to knock the dollar off the top of the global currency mountain where it now sits.

CHAPTER 79

WHAT A COUNTRY

When Facebook went public in 2012, a great debate raged regarding the viability of an investment in this newly public company. Could the company really be worth the $100 billion that it was being valued at in its initial public offering? Could it be worth a lot more? Are small investors crazy to invest at the IPO? These were all valid questions at the time, but most people were missing the point and a sense of the larger picture. The beauty of the Facebook IPO, or any IPO for that matter, is that they happen at all. The grand sense of possibility and uncertainty of a new stock offering is what this country is all about and has always been about.

At the very founding of our new nation in 1776, we were a ragtag group of underdogs whose members craved more than the world offered them. It was a group that saw endless possibilities where others only saw the inevitability of the status quo. It is absolutely no coincidence that most of the world's great inventions, from the light bulb to the airplane to the computer to the Polio vaccine, arose from American ingenuity and the entrepreneurial spirit of its people. A populace with no hope is not very inventive. People armed with optimism and dreams, people who can stumble off into the void of uncertainty, invent great things. The Facebook IPO allowed us to celebrate not the wealth that was being created, but the marketplace itself that allowed such optimism, innovation, and ambition to flourish.

In 2002, three of the largest companies in the world by market value today were in their infancies. Apple was just rolling out its newfangled iPod product, and the company only had a market value of $6 billion. Google was still tiny and not publicly traded, and Facebook was not even a glimmer in Mark Zuckerberg's eye. Today, a mere seventeen years later, the market value of these three companies totals more than $2.4 trillion and is growing every day. In fact, 70 percent of Apple's profits now come from a product that was not even introduced until 2007. Now that is a dynamic, innovative, fast-changing economy.

The Facebook IPO reminded investors vividly of the Google IPO in 2004. Then, as now, potential investors were analyzing a company that was short on revenue and profits and long on possibility. At its IPO, Google had earned forty-one cents a share in 2003 and had estimated its earnings of $1 per share for 2004. At the IPO price of $85, or 85-times forward earnings, the company appeared very richly valued indeed. Investors and the media endlessly debated the wisdom or insanity of investing in a company valued so highly and how fast the company would have to grow revenue and earnings to justify that price.

The IPO was successful anyway and investors took the plunge. What investors at the time could not have known was that Google would earn $2 a share in 2004, $5.33 in 2005, and $9.94 a share in 2006. In hindsight, IPO investors were paying only 9-times earnings, two years out, for a fabulous company that went on to earn $32.80 a share in 2011 and $54.75 a share in 2018. Google's inventors and investors saw endless possibilities where its detractors saw risk, peril, and downside. Uncertainty is what makes markets and is what makes America great. Our 330 million Americans are a diverse group with extremely varied views of politics, business, and lifestyle choices. However, in the never-ending race to create things that advance society and make the world a better place, you can take the best 330 million people from the rest of the world, and put them up against ours, and I will bet on our 330 million to win the race every time.

Facebook's fortunes might have quickly flamed out like AOL, or Research in Motion, or WebVan. History is full of bright stars that burn out quickly. Could an investor have based an investment in Facebook on the valuation of that year's current numbers? Absolutely not. However, investors did know that the founders had done an amazing job creating a very valuable something-out-of-nothing idea. They also knew that there were thousands of brilliant people at Facebook working long hours to create new products and services that could grow the company in the future.

More importantly for our economy, investors knew that the success of Facebook would spark a thousand new ideas for a thousand new companies and products. Some will succeed and most will fail gloriously. Fortunately, America has a culture that celebrates new ideas and risk-taking and a people that are the hardest working, most entrepreneurial, and most innovative in the world. That spirit will lead to the creation of other great companies that we have not heard of yet by founders that we will only get to know in the future. They will be inventing products that we did not even know we needed.

Words of the Wise: What will our world look like ten years from now? I have no idea, and that is an amazing thing. Old companies and ideas will fail, and new ones will rise to take their places. Our American future is uncertain. And we should not want it any other way.

EPILOGUE

One of my favorite movie quotes is from the opening scene of *Annie Hall*. Alvy Singer (Woody Allen) tells a story. Alvy says, "There's an old joke. Two elderly women are at a Catskills Mountains resort, and one of the women says, 'You know, the food here is really terrible.' And the other woman says, 'Yes, I know, and such small portions!' Well, that is essentially how I feel about life. Full of loneliness, misery, suffering, and unhappiness. And it's all over much too quickly."

While Allen's character in the movie was famously neurotic, fatalistic, and morose, the underlying reflection still shines through. Life can at times be challenging, joyous, exhilarating, frustrating, sad, fulfilling, and overwhelming. And it goes very fast and is all over much too quickly.

I wrote this book to share a lifetime of lessons learned, money burned, and scars earned. And hopefully it works as a map with shortcuts around the bumps in the road that you will face. When I was a child, I wanted to be an adult because then I would have all the answers to both everyday problems and life's big questions. I was disappointed to later learn that adults don't in fact have all the answers. They strive and struggle everyday just as young adults do.

But I do know a couple of things for sure…

As you get older and look back on your life, the regrets that you will have will center on the things you could have done but didn't do. You will give very little thought to the shame or guilt of the stupid things that you did do.

Money that you earn yourself will mean much more to you and generate far more pride than money that is just handed to you, unearned.

Always spend the extra money to buy a great mattress. You will forget what you paid for it in a few days, and you will sleep well on it for ten years.

And finally, marry someone who you would be just as happy living in a storage bin with as in a mansion. Marry someone who you would jump in front of a train for and who would do the same for you. Marry someone who knows if your mood is off by just 1 percent, even before you do, and who asks how they can help. And never let them go.

Good luck!

ACKNOWLEDGEMENTS

My many thanks go out to all the people who made this book possible:

My fabulous editor, Carrie Jones, who can polish coal into diamonds. Carrie is a young adult fiction author and a New York Times bestselling author of the *Need* series, *Time Stoppers* series, and *Flying* series of novels. Carrie attended Bates College in my hometown of Lewiston, Maine, and now lives in Bar Harbor, Maine. Find out more about her writings, life and rescue animals at www.carriejonesbooks.com.

My esteemed webmaster and website creator, Chris Pillsbury. See examples of his stellar work at www.pillsburycreative.com.

The fine folks at BookBaby who took charge of every phase of this book's production, from Word manuscript to final format and printing.

Many thanks to my parents, Jim and Muriel MacDonald, for always teaching, pushing and encouraging me over the many years of my life. I could never lose my way in a storm with such strong, bright and steadfast beacons always lighting the way.

Thanks to my loving and thoughtful sisters, Shirley Freeman and Jennifer Mulholland. They have always been with me through good times and bad, with good advice and strong shoulders.

A sincere shout out to my friend and mentor Susan Byrne, whom I worked side by side with at Westwood Management for 25 years. Susan made her way and came of age in the sharp-elbowed Wall Street men's club of the early 1970s. There were not many doors open to a young, single mother at the time, so she just cut a hole in the wall, walked through and staked her own claim. Susan was one of the first women on Wall Street to found her own asset management firm, which she then deftly stewarded over the next thirty-five years. Her wise counsel, wisdom and confidence in me over the decades will always be treasured.

Many thanks to Chip Marz for his continual interest in my journey and writings, and his constant encouragement to keep pushing forward to produce good work. And to drink good beer.

And if you have an interest in writing, publishing and editing, or just enjoy interesting podcasts, visit thecreativepenn.com and listen to Joanna Penn's podcast *The Creative Penn* on iTunes. Joanna is a fantastic teacher, and her voice is like a bucket of sunshine poured into a cup of morning coffee. She has recorded more than 400 editions of her podcast and is still going strong.

NOTES

Chapter 1 – Quote by John Henry Cardinal Newman (1801-1890), on aquina-sandmore.com. Material on the quality vs. quantity theory of art creation was inspired by *Art & Fear: Observations on the Perils (and Rewards) of Artmaking*, by David Bayles and Ted Orland. (Image Continuum Press, 2001). The Picasso story has been passed down over many years, but was found at www.1099.com/c/ar/ta/HowToCharge_t042.html.

Chapter 2 – The fascinating lecture by Steph Curry can be viewed at Masterclass. com. The lectures by bestselling thriller authors Dan Brown and David Baldacci are timeless as well.

Chapter 4 – The quote is often attributed to Winston Churchill, but academics have widely noted that there is no evidence of this original source. I liked the quote however, even if the original source has been lost to time.

Chapter 5 – The story of Vivien Maier was detailed in *Why the Collectors Who Made Vivian Maier Famous Can't Cash in on Her Work,* by Jessica Meiselman. (Artsy.com, July 11, 2017). With additional inspiration from *Vivian Maier: Street Photographer*, by John Maloof. (powerHouse Books, 2012).

Chapter 7 – Details of the strange but true east side/west side city settlement came from *East Side Story: Historical Pollution and Persistent Neighborhood Sorting*, by Stephen Heblich, Alex Trew and Yanos Zylberberg. (University of St. Andrews School of Economics and Finance Discussion Pages, 2018).

Chapter 9 – Quote is from *The Last Lecture* by Randy Pausch. (Hyperion, 2008). Dan Brown, author of *The Da Vinci Code*, told the story of his meeting with Steven Tyler in his lecture for *Masterclass,* at Masterclass.com.

Chapter 10 – A major contribution to the knowledge and discussion of superstars and their effect on consumer economics came from *The Economics of Superstars*, by Sherwin Rosen. (The American Economic Review, 1981).

Chapter 11 – The discussion on academic achievement draws heavily on the research report *Academic Achievement A View from the Top. The Illinois Valedictorian Project*, by Karen D. Arnold. (North Central Regional Educational Lab, 1993). I would recommend a recent book *Barking Up the Wrong Tree*, by Eric Barker. (HarperOne, 2017), which also detailed the work of Karen Arnold.

Chapter 14 – Details about the fascinating history of glass in this chapter was derived primarily from the fascinating book *How We Got To Now: Six Innovations That Made the Modern World*, by Steven Johnson. (Riverhead Books, 2015).

Chapter 17 – Milton Friedman's discussions with Phil Donahue are fascinating and timeless viewing and can be found on YouTube at *Milton Friedman on Donahue 1979* and *Milton Friedman on Donahue #2.*

Chapter 18 – A wealth of NBA scoring statistics can be found at teamrankings. com/nba

Chapter 19 – Many of the ideas and quotations about the Vanderbilt family, its players and its history in this chapter come from the book *Fortune's Children: The Fall of the House of Vanderbilt*, by Arthur T. Vanderbilt II. (WmMorrowPB, 1991). It is a fascinating read which covers the rise and fall of this great American family in page-turning detail.

Chapter 20 – The website cureblindess.org provides a wealth of information on the organization, its good works, and its founders. Additional information can be found by reading *In 5 Minutes, He Lets the Blind See*, by Nicholas Kristof. (The New York Times, Nov. 7, 2015). Patient quote from *Eye opening: Curing Cataracts in the Himalayas and Beyond*, by Emma Hiolski. (Stanford Medicine, 2017).

Chapter 21 – Information and ideas about the fascinating world of ransom and hostage negotiation from this chapter rely heavily on the teachings and career of Chris Voss, as told in his book *Never Split the Difference – Negotiating as if Your Life Depended On It*. (Harper Business, 2016). I recommend it highly for the details of his wealth of experience and his lessons for life, business and sealing a deal.

Chapter 22 – Chris Hadfield's lecture on space travel, exploration and his life journey can be found on Masterclass.com. Chris is my favorite teacher on Masterclass, and his thoughts and experiences are not to be missed.

Chapter 23 – Read more about network effects at *What Are Network Effects?*, by Nicholas L. Johnson. (Applico, Feb. 15, 2018), and *The Power of Network Effects: Why They Make Such Valuable Companies, and How to Harness Them*, by Eric Jorgenson. (Medium, June 22, 2015).

Chapter 24 – Extensive information on professor Ignacio Palacios-Huerta, the noted expert on soccer statistics, and his many works can be found at www.palacios-huerta.com/index.html. Zero-sum quote and other soccer game theory ideas can be found at *Explaining Soccer Shot-Making with Game Theory,* by GianCarlo Moschini. (Soccermetrics.net, 2009).

Chapter 25 – Some of the details of the life story of Diana Hendricks came from *Meet America's Richest Self-Made Woman,* by Jennifer Calfas. (Money Magazine, October 5, 2018). Also by Diana's comments in *The Business Must Go On,* as told to Amy Zipkin. (The New York Times, Nov. 21, 2009), and *In Weary Wisconsin Town, a Billionaire-Fueled Revival,* by Alexander Stevenson. (The New York Times, August 5, 2017). Nelson Mandela quote can be found in *Mandela: The Authorized Biography,* by Anthony Sampson. (Vintage, 2000).

Chapter 27 – The fascinating and surprising history of house numbers explained in this chapter came primarily from the book *House Numbers: Pictures of a Forgotten History* by Anton Tantner. (Reaktion Books, 2016). Additional information came from *Where the Streets Have No Names, the People Have No Vote,* by Deirdre Mask. (*The New York Times,* October 19, 2018).

Chapter 29 – Extensive information about the life and works of Milton Friedman and be found at www.cato.org/special/friedman/friedman/index.html.

Chapter 31 – The Warren Buffett age switch question was detailed by Nick Maggiulli is his always thought-provoking Dollars and Data blog (ofdollarsanddata.com, July 17, 2018). Quotes also from *The Top Five Regrets of the Dying: A Life Transformed by the Dearly Departing,* by Bronnie Ware. (Hay House Inc., 2012).

Chapter 33 – Quotes from Volcker and Siegel and details on the history of inflation in the United States can be studied by reading *The Great Inflation: A Historical Overview and Lessons Learned,* by David A. Lopez. (Federal Reserve Bank of St. Louis, 2012).

Chapter 34 – The Big Rocks story is told by Stephen Covey at www.appleseeds.org/Big-Rocks_Covey.htm. Learn more about Stephen Covey and the work of Franklin Covey at Franklincovey.com. And read *The 7 Habits of Highly Effective People: Powerful Lessons in Personal Change,* by Stephen Covey. (DC Books, 1994).

Chapter 36 – See *The Social Conquest of Earth,* by Edward O. Wilson. (Liveright, 2013).

Chapter 37 – See *What is a Recession?,* by Kimberly Amadeo. (The Balance, Oct. 1, 2018). And *What is a Recession?,* by Bill Connerly. (Forbes, Nov. 29, 2016).

Chapter 39 – Details on how many books a year that CEOs read came from *Most CEOs Read a Book a Week. This is How You Can Too,* by Brian Evans. (Inc. magazine, June 27, 2017).

Chapter 40 – See *The Geopolitics of the United States, Part 1: The Inevitable Empire* at Stratfor.com.

Chapter 42 – Read more about the Nixon scandal in *Watergate: The Presidential Scandal That Shook America,* by Max Holland. (University Press of Kansas, 2016). And *Bringing Down A President: The Watergate Scandal,* by Andrea Balls and Elizabeth Levy (Roaring Book Press, 2019).

Chapter 45 – Learn more about the history, economic role and responsibilities of the Federal Reserve at federalreserve.gov.

Chapter 47 – Some ideas on NATO's history and positive role in furthering global security came from *Europe's Dependence on the U.S. Was All Part of the Plan,* by Claire Berlinski. (Politico Magazine, 2018).

Chapter 50 – Keynes quote from *The General Theory of Employment, Interest, and Money* by John Maynard Keynes. (Amazon POD, 2018).

Chapter 52 – For more information on the long and winding road of U.S. and Cuba relations see Council on Foreign Relations at cfr.org/backgrounder/us-cuba-relations. And *The Cuban Revolution and resistance to the United States,* by Louis A. Perez Jr. (OUP Blog, Dec. 13, 2016).

Chapter 53 – See *Stocks for the Long Run,* by Jeremy Siegel. (McGraw Hill, 2014).

Chapter 54 – To read more about Grace Groner, see *Secret millionaire donates fortune to Lake Forest College* by John Keilman. (Chicago Tribune, March 5, 2010). And *How a Secretary Made and Gave Away $7 Million,* by Robert Frank. (The Wall Street Journal, March 8, 2010).

Chapter 57 – Quote is from *Embrace Your Magnificence: Get Out of Your Own Way and Live a Richer, Fuller, More Abundant Life,* by Fabienne Fredrickson. (Balboa Press, 2013).

Chapter 59 – Quotes and information on the life and journey of Muriel Seibert can be found in *Senior Women Web Interviews Muriel Seibert,* at Seniorwomen. com.

Chapter 60 – Please see *Do 'Close Door' Buttons in Elevators Actually Do Anything?,* by Emily Petsko. (Mentalfloss.com, June 22, 2018)

Chapter 61 – The hypothetical discussion between a customer and a grocer came from *Boycotts and Prices,* by Milton Friedman. (Newsweek, November 28, 1966).

Chapter 62 - *Enlightenment Now*, by Steven Pinker. (Penguin Group USA, 2019). Pinker's many lecture videos on YouTube and TED.com are very entertaining, and highly recommended. The Adams quote is recently attributed to him, but the original source is widely debated.

Chapter 66 – Timber investment content from *Thousands of Southerners Planted Trees for Retirement. It Didn't Work*, by Ryan Dezember. (The Wall Street Journal, Oct. 9, 2018).

Chapter 67 – Truman quote on containment of Communism from The Truman Doctrine, adopted as U.S. policy in 1947. For more information on the Cold War, visit *history.com/topics/cold-war/cold-war-history*, by History.com editors. And jfklibrary.org.

Chapter 68 – Quote on Julian Robertson is from *The End of the Game; Tiger Management, Old-Economy Advocate, Is Closing*, by Gretchen Morgenson. (The New York Times, March 31, 2000).

Chapter 69 – For timeless wisdom on wealth management, read *Simple Wealth, Inevitable Wealth*, by Nick Murray. (The Nick Murray Company Inc., 1999)

Chapter 70 – Read more about the history of the bread slicing machine at *The Invention of Sliced Bread*, by Zachary Crockett. (Priceonomics, Nov. 12, 2014). *The greatest thing since...*, by Margot Peppers. (Daily Mail, July 8, 2013).

Chapter 72 – More raw data on fertility rates can be found at ourworldindata. org/fertility-rate

Chapter 74 – Information for the perils of the year 536 can be found in *Why 536 Was the Worst Year to be Alive,* by Ann Gibbons. (Science magazine, Nov. 15, 2018). *You Think 2018 is the Worst Year Ever?*, by Kate Williams. (The Guardian, Nov. 23, 2018).

Chapter 76 – Predictions on the future of Amazon were reported in *Amazon.bomb* in Barron's magazine, May 31, 1999.

Chapter 77 – More information about how our right and left road driving standards evolved can be found at www.worldstandards.eu/cars/driving-on-the-left/.

Chapter 78 – Information on the history and rise of the dollar and the currency market in general came from *Exorbitant Privilege: The Rise and Fall of the Dollar and the Future of the International Monetary System*, by Barry Eichengreen. (Oxford University Press, 2012).

Some chapters of this work are used by permission from ©Westwood Holdings Group, Inc. These include chapters: 1, 2, 5, 7, 10, 13, 16, 19, 20, 21, 22, 23, 25, 27, 28, 29, 30, 33, 36, 42, 47, 58, 61.